Just a

This book is taken from a video series – Andy B 2 Minute Videos, which you can find online at www.berrybunch.family, or you can use the QR code.

The BerryBunch create digital material - to encourage and inspire families, all around the world, in their Christian faith; supporting, equipping and resourcing the Church in its Global mission: for free, for all.

All websites listed herein are correct at the time of publishing, but these may change in the future, or cease to function. Links to other websites does not constitute, or imply, endorsement of that site's entire contents.

Dedication

Just a Thought… was born out of my Andy B 2 Minute Videos.

I'm not one who is well known for being brief. So, I set myself a challenge of filming a short video of anything 2 minutes 59 seconds or less. And, thus, Andy B 2 Minute Videos came to life.

So, to everybody who has watched, viewed, liked, commented and shared my Andy B 2 Minute Videos, and encouraged me - thank you!

Nathan – thanks for the grammar checks. Most helpful!

Jo – you're a very understanding, and brilliant example of Proverbs 31 wife who's light shines ever brighter in the dark. Thanks for your ever present encouragement since we met in the 1990s. You never let me stay down for long!

Johnny – your effervescent zest for life is wonderfully, and reassuringly, overwhelming and refreshing.

Andy B

Foreword

Everything in a person flows out of their heart. The whole of life is heart work flowing from enlivened thoughts. Truly thoughts matter!

Jesus said you would know a tree by its fruit. The fruit of a tree is a consequence of the root it's connected to. An orange can never come from an apple tree root. The core of who you are is evidenced by your life thinking and actions resulting. That's why what is on the inside is so much more important than what is on the outside. Interior work matters. You can temporarily mask, bury, or fake the veneer of your world, but one day it will show.

Ultimately, what's in your heart will reveal who you are.

Little, daily and consistent choices shape it all. Little thoughts, anchored to bigger truths, for a flourishing God-sense life!

The thoughts and inclinations of the heart shape the reality of who you and I are. They shape our thinking, which ultimately shapes our actions. So this book is about more than thoughts. It's about ordering our lives under the good grace of God in the mix of this brilliant and broken world.

The disarming invitation of this book is that we might "let God run some diagnostics as you listen to the Holy Spirit!"

This book is a fizzy bundle of word-full, picture-rich, kingdom-shaped possibilities! Whole-life discipleship, lived-theology, and grown-up experience rings true here in vivid detail and radiant colour.

Andy offers us a collision of the ordinary and unexpected in the beckoning of Jesus in the power of the Holy Spirit. Just a Thought… is "a collection of pregnant brain thoughts." But it's so much more than this. Andy reflects a determination, character, and grasp of God in His loving purpose and wise ways.

Thoughts are the incubation unit for the firing pattern of neurons, which eventually leads to a new way of being.

Proverbs 23:7 captures an enduring truth when it says, "As a person thinks, so they are!" So may the thoughts of our lips and the lived truths of our hearts be truly *pleasing in your sight. For you, Lord, are my Rock and my Redeemer!*

Revd Johnny Douglas

Just a thought…

2 Minutes a Day Can Change Your World

Contents

Say What?
An introduction?

To the many people that know me well, my random thoughts seem normal. Or so I keep telling myself. After all, we all have them, don't we? We accept that a pregnant woman may well desire the weirdest of food combinations, and it makes sense, after all.

Sweet and Sour – one example of two things that shouldn't go together, but just do. Grapes and sugar is another one. Also, cliffs and home – well, if you're English, and you're on a ferry coming home to England.

We all put things together that don't make much sense. My favourite toasted sandwich is Bovril and Tuna Fish…because it just makes sense.

Just a Thought… is a collection of my pregnant brain thoughts. Only I'm not female. You get the idea, no?

It's sort of like a devotional with a topic per day to get your brain working, that refers back to faith in one way or another, and usually via a route never expected. Think of this as your earlier morning stretching, but to get those kinks out of your mind.

You can think of me as the Shackleton of brain thoughts. Or the Christopher Columbus…ooh potatoes…I'm hungry again.

Just a Thought… is better than a caffeine shot – which I don't drink anymore due to a heart that is a drama queen. Actually, thinking about it, my lack of caffeine has led to an abundance of Andy B 2 Minute Videos, from which this book finds its roots.

Anyway, if you're ready to expand your mind, or just get it warmed up, read on.

Andy B

1. 50% Connected is NOT Fully Connected

We once lived in a very rural location, where normal internet connections simply didn't exist. There were, literally, no serviceable landlines to connect to our home. So, we started using a local Radio Broadband service instead.

Having fallen in love with the simplicity of getting our internet provided to us, cable free, we stuck with it and have been using a 4G Router in our home ever since.

When COVID hit the UK in 2020 we invested in a second internet connection for my wife's working from home. We also bought a rechargeable Mobile Router.

On the side of that Mobile Router there are two rather small silver things sticking out from the main unit, covered by a small plastic flap, which is where you can choose to plug in an external aerial.

I bought the correct aerials and connections, plugged them in, and off we went! Or so I thought.

I began to get pretty frustrated that, no matter what I did, the reception was still pretty rubbish. I started to think that the router, or the aerials, must be defective. However, before returning it, I thought I'd check out which part of the chain was faulty.

If you remember the TV aerials of old, you may well remember having to hold it in various, odd places, around the house to get a good enough picture. Well, I started moving my mobile router around the room in the same way, but to no joy.

When that failed, I started checking there was an internet signal for it to even find. And out of frustration, I started waving it around the room. It was at this point that one of the aerials fell out!

It was also at this point that I realised that aside from looking rather foolish to anybody looking through my bedroom window, that I may have found the issue!

Because it turned out that one of the aerials was barely plugged in, while the other was so badly plugged in that it actually fell out and took up flying instead.

As much as those aerials worked well, I hadn't actually plugged them in fully.

It struck me – how often with God are we, similarly, not actually plugged in to Him?

We go to church, so we assume we've got one of those aerials plugged in – because we're turning up to the building. But, we're still only, perhaps, just 50% of the way there. We may well be in the church building, but we're not really listening because we're not actually plugged in mentally!

We're sitting in the church, with a Bible in our lap, but thinking that nobody else sees the bulletin that sits just inside it that we're really reading instead. So it looks like we're plugged in to the sermon, and the church but, really, we're not. Which puts us in the same place as the aerials and my router! We're barely plugged in.

This made me think about our daily lives – are you reading your Bible every day, but just going through the motions? Are you reading the words in black and white before you, but not letting them sink into your heart?

Are you praying to God, but forgetting that prayer is a two-way conversation and, just like any other conversation, you need to be speaking out, as well as listening in.

Are you fully plugged in? Or do you just look like you're fully plugged in? Have you pushed your connection towards God to make it look good for others? Or are you pushing towards God with all of you, and what you are, so you can be fully connected to, and with, God?

Let's pray and read our bibles. But let's make sure we're fully connected to God. Let's allow those words to enter our mind and our hears and bodies.

Otherwise, we'll just end up wandering around our lives, trying to hold that aerial in the air, finding all sorts of contorted positions to try and get the better signal, and getting nothing more than snow on the TV screen of our lives.

Just a thought…

2. Bananas, Eggs And Corn On The Cob

Genesis 1, verse 11 says this:

> *And God said, "Let the earth sprout vegetation, plants yielding seed, and fruit trees bearing fruit in which is their seed, each according to its kind, on the earth." And it was so.*

The great thing about the book of Genesis is that God is telling us how He made the world we know and love. And what a world! We see in those words how God, literally, speaks the earth into being.

And while cooking dinner one evening, I had a thought about bananas, eggs, and corn on the cob. Because during the first UK lockdown, germs were rather on my mind because I'd been to the supermarket and bought these things!

What troubled me was a memory about how, a long time ago, I had been doing some industrial drilling, and we were drilling through 25-year-old domestic household waste, from houses in Edinburgh, Scotland.

It was my first job after leaving school, and wasn't my favourite ever job, I'll be honest.

I'm not going to describe what I saw, smelt, and had to deal with during those 10 long days, but I did learn one important life skill and lesson – what foods you can eat, with a pair of gloves, without actually having to touch your food. Because, when you're suited up in protective clothing, for 14 hours a day, and you want to eat – but don't want to repeatedly climb in and out of that protective clothing – it's amazing what you can learn to do! Necessity really is the mother of invention.

And this is one reason why you can get really good at opening plastic packets of food with your mouth and pouring the food in, without ever actually touching it!

With COVID being something of a new thing in the world through 2019 onwards, we bought these foods in the supermarket, washed them, and they then went into our bath to be quarantined.

Now, the great thing about corn on the cob is that it comes into our homes already COVID safe – when you bring it home, it is already, safely, wrapped. And the really fabulous thing about corn on the cob is that you take off the outer layer – the husk – and you've got a perfectly formed and protected vegetable.

With its outer wrapper, you get a food item, free of germs.

And what about eggs? Another great design from God, just like corn on the cob – something else that comes pre-wrapped and perfectly packaged for us.

All of this got me thinking about the many complicated methods we've built up and constructed, when God already made so many things for us, that are far simpler.

God spoke the world into existence, but He also designed some really awesome things. Like eggs! He made them so that we didn't have to worry about Covid-19 being on our food. He made bananas with stuff on the outside to protect the fruit inside. Although, we've learned not to eat the skin, 'cos that really isn't very nice and won't end well!

There are so many things that God has put in place for us.

Sometimes, I think that in life we're trying really, really hard to come up with really complicated end results so that we can say that that was our design.

So, what does plastic packaging have in common with bananas that come germ free?

Well, eggs, bananas, and corn on the cob all have one thing in common – the simple solution God designed with them having an outer skin, protecting them from all sorts of things.

In life we can become quite adept at seeking out complicated solutions.

But let's appreciate the simplicity of design that God built into the things He designed. Because sometimes the simplest things are right in front of our faces.

Just a thought…

3. Saucepan Lids, Discipline and Walking In God's Strength

So, I was doing a spot of cooking for my family, and I had a thought, as I often do, about Hebrews 12, verse 7.

> *"It is for discipline that you have to endure. God is treating you as sons. For what son is there whom his father does not discipline?" (English Standard Version)*

I was thinking about that and also Jeremiah 29, verse 11, as I was looking at boiling some pasta for dinner!

Now, Jeremiah 29, verse 11 is a fairly well-known piece of Scripture, although it's often not known for what it actually means:

"For I know the plans I have for you, declares the Lord, plans for welfare and not for evil, to give you a future and a hope." (English Standard Version)

Now, if you have the lid off the pasta you have to have the heat on really high, or the water just won't boil as easily. And pasta needs to be boiled, not gently heated! I've tried cooking it slowly, over a low heat, and it simply doesn't turn out the same.

If you put on the saucepan lid, all of a sudden, you're creating a low-pressure system, which means you can turn the heat down. Otherwise, you have boiling water, saturated with the starch from the pasta, spreading itself all over your kitchen top and floor.

When you put that lid on, completely, you have to have that heat REALLY low. But, you don't need much heat – combined with a lid – to boil the water and the pasta.

If you're anything like my family you will, over time, experiences seasons when you feel like you're being restricted by God, similar to the cries of Bruce Almighty, in the film of the same name.

You'll quite possibly find yourself in a place where you're thinking, "God, why can't I do more than I'm doing?"

Maybe you, like the character in Bruce Almighty, feel like there is 'an anti-Bruce barrier' or an anti-[enter your surname here] barrier.

It struck me that this is a little bit like what we read in that Jeremiah passage above – chapter 29, verse 11.

If the Lord wants us to be prosperous, and give us really good lives, why does it sometimes feel as though we're really stuck at one particular point in life, with a roof we cannot push beyond?!? And the whole time thinking that there has to be something bad going on against us: conspiracy theorists unite!!

What may feel like an 'anti-you' barrier, could just as easily be God putting some limits around you, because He cares enough to try and prevent you from exhausting yourself from running at life, full pelt. Or, for example, cranking up the gas on your kitchen stove to boil the pasta with no lid on, when there's an equally quick, simpler, cheaper solution?

Because, actually, God might be putting a lid on you to try and make you focus more on what He is trying to help you achieve. And because, actually, it's the quicker route to where He wants you to reach.

So, if you feel like we have felt as a family, many times, know you're in very good company!

And, also, remember that the barrier you feel restricting you may not be something designed to stop you making progress, but to help you reach the goal, just with less effort.

So be encouraged, and maybe turn the gas down on your stove, and add a lid. And let's let God's restrictions grow us and shape us – it's much less tiring after all.

Just a thought…

4. Humble or Proud?

I was writing a story for our online baby and toddler group –Little Blessings Online – and we were looking at the feeding of the 5,000.

So, I sat there thinking, "OK, how can I get into this? How can I get into the story? How can I move from southern England, in the UK, to a pretty desolate group of people who were starving in the Middle East?"

And, so, I read the account of The Feeding of the 5,000, in Matthew 14, and also the same account of this amazing miracle where it appears in John, chapter 6. And it really struck me – about what was also going on, specifically that John had just been beheaded by Herod. At this point, Jesus then goes away, to be alone, 'cos He's sad.

And it's also at this point that the feeding of the 5,000 happens!

It's within a portion of the Bible that is really very sad, before we move on to an amazing miracle.

Jesus has to switch from mourning for over loss of His friend, to taking some much needed time alone and on to feeding 5,000 hungry people.

And, of course, just to make it an even greater challenge, there are around 5,000 men recorded. But some of those men would have also had with them their wives and their children too. Which puts the number, conservatively, somewhere around the 20,000 hungry-people-to-feed mark!

In Matthew's gospel it talks about a time when Jesus walked on water. And when the disciples saw Jesus, they thought that He was actually a ghost – they thought that Jesus was dead. And death is pretty much all around the middle of these two passages of Scripture, and moments and feelings of death and darkness and hopelessness.

You've got these two accounts of Jesus feeding 5,000 [plus] and it tells us, in John's gospel, about how "perceiving that they were about to come and take him by force to make him King, Jesus withdrew".

So, John has been beheaded. Jesus is really sad, and He goes up a mountain, and then borrows some lunch from a young boy – which is going to be the story I'm writing. And what struck me about all this is a question: when God does something good, do we think, "Yes, I've done something good for God"? Or, instead, do we actually think "Yeah, God has done something amazing for me."

Putting this another way, are we prone to saying that "God is good" only when things are going well for us? Or do we say that "God is good" and that God has done this whether we think things are going well or not.

Are we making ourselves look good, or God?

Just a thought…

5. Boats, Shops and Resting

I was sitting with a cup of tea in our car in a car park. I was waiting for my wife, Jo, who needed to visit a satellite office to print out a large document.

As I'm quietly sat there in that little car park, next to me is a small Marina, on the south coast of the UK. There are little boats and some larger boats.

Now I'm not much into boats myself otherwise I'd tell you the types of boats that I was looking at: my personal experience in the boating fraternity is limited to mastering the oars on a tiny rowboat in a very small lake at an inner-city park. But I do know enough to name the boat I can see. It's called a very big boat!

It's actually a very large cruise liner, and it got me thinking about holidays, about resting and about being on a cruise liner a long time ago, and sailing across to Denmark to go to Legoland.

It was a great trip and I got to experience plenty of moments to rest on that boat as we crossed the North Sea over to Denmark!

But do we rest at other times? Do you rest? Personally, I'm extremely, and highly proficient, at not resting! I'm just as skilled at not getting to bed on time. Does the phrase 'burning the candle at both ends' mean anything to you?

How about 'burning the candle at both ends, and in the middle? We've all done that, haven't we – burning the candle at both ends? There are some seasons in life when we simply have to get stuff done and keep going, even if it means working through the night, skipping our sleep and shooting out to work the next morning.

As we were doing some filming for another BerryBunch project I was recording a piece which looked at John's gospel, chapter 1. We were looking at "the word". We were looking at 'who is the word?' And that led me to thinking about how Jesus was an "agent of creation". Before long I found myself in the book of Genesis – one of my favourite books in the Bible – looking at God creating the world.

The opening chapters of Genesis are some of my favourite because they assure me that the God whom I love was, and is, and will always be. It reminds me that God's words, and His Word, are absolutely trustworthy.

And as I was sitting there next to that small Marina, looking at the boats, I was having some 'passive resting'. I was deliberately sitting there, relaxed, and on purpose, looking at the boats in the Marina and listening to the clinking from the masts and the sound of the rain on the roof of the car. Which all led me to thinking about seasons of life, and the importance of rhythm.

Because God did exactly that. God worked to a rhythm! He had these six, full on days of working – creating the world and everything in it, including the 4 seasons. But then God takes off the 7th day to have a day of rest.

And that, right there, is the rhythm we all follow every week on our calendars, and in our places of work. And it matches that rhythm which God set for us when He made the world.

God didn't need to rest – He is God after all! But if God took time out to rest, then we should too!

And God didn't work overnight either. The Bible tells us that "there was evening, then morning." It tells us that God only made things during daylight hours – so we can rest assured that sleeping is a good thing. So, make sure you get some rest!

Take time to rest passively and take time to rest actively.

But get in that rest!

Just a thought…

6. Booster Seats and Blockages

Like parents all around the world, we've needed to use booster seats in our cars for our children – to keep them safe. Booster seats come in all sorts of shapes and sizes and have one real job, to keep our children safe in the case of an accident.

Some booster seats come with a full back, and head support. Some are literally just sufficient to lift the child high enough so that the seat belt doesn't rub against their neck and so it can perform its job if we ever have to come to a dramatic stop.

With 3 children we've always struggled to find a car in the UK wide enough to safely accommodate both them and 3 booster seats. But it came to the moment when Peter, our youngest son, stated – emphatically – that he no longer needed a booster seat, because his brothers didn't need one.

After a chat about British Law, and how it doesn't quite work that way, we measured his height and weight to ensure we could purchase the correct booster seat. Only to discover that, as we have often found with Peter, he was right! Because he had grown tall enough so that he didn't need a booster seat.

Our very last booster seat was purchased because of one unique and specific feature. It was super narrow, which made life easier placing it between two older children. This booster seat was actually an inflatable booster seat.

To be honest, it didn't last especially well, and we had to have it replaced, under warrantee, in less than 8 months. Our next one didn't last much longer! As with all things that can be inflated, they can be de-inflated too, even when you don't want them to be. Also, unlike bicycle tyres, they can't be repaired at home.

Back when Peter still needed his booster seat it didn't help that, unbeknown to us, the blow-up seat was losing its ability to hold air. It was losing enough air that while we couldn't easily tell when we checked it, it was more than enough to make it not fit for purpose.

If you need a booster seat for a child, then you need it to work. There's no point in having one that can be inflated but can't retain the air you carefully blew into it! And this made me think about our lives.

Perhaps you're struggling through some things in your life, and you think you need some help. We all do at various times in our lives!

For Peter, sitting in the car safely meant we needed a booster seat that allowed for 3 bottoms to sit side by side. This was harder than it first looked! Our solution to stay legal while driving, and keep him safe, was a blow-up booster seat. When it worked it was brilliant! When he'd outgrown the need for it, there was no longer any point in him sitting on it.

When those things that we're relying upon in our lives don't work we need to take some action.

Peter's blow-up booster seat was relied upon, and very important. But it simply wasn't doing what we thought it was.

We have things like this in our lives – things we rely on which we know are really important, but we also know do not work and no amount of blowing air into them is going to help.

Sometimes we need to spend a little time with those things undergoing a spot of maintenance. But sometimes we just need to cut them loose, and get rid of them.

Just a thought…

7. Washing Machine Gaskets and God

Washing machine gaskets. They can have a few different names depending on what language you speak or where you are in the world, and depending on what your washing machine maker decided to call them. But their purpose is simply to prevent water from leaving your washing machine onto the floor in front of it.

They have one job to do – when you close the door, they create a good seal so water in the machine doesn't leak out. Our washing machine gasket failed.

Over time they dry out, becoming less flexible. We'd bought our washing machine brand new, and it had been heavily used by this family of 5 for around three years. So how had it failed?

Under closer inspection, while trying not to see my lunch reappear, from the smells coming from it, I noticed that it had a perfectly smooth form and profile all the way around, except for two parts where the rubber was sticking out at an odd angle at two points at the top.

It only became a problem when the machine started spinning, forcing water higher up the door, out through the deformed parts of the seal, down the door and underneath.

Thankfully, we saw that tiny trickle – mostly because our water was known as 'hard water', which meant it had a very high concentration of limescale. This formed a crust as it settled, which was easy to see. So, we ordered a new part, I fitted it, and all was good again.

In each of our lives we have those same, almost unrecognisable, deformities that only become a problem when we're under pressure.

So, where in your life have you got important gaskets that are protecting you from things escaping that shouldn't?

Will we trust our master Craftsman – our Creator God – to come along and change those seals which are letting out what shouldn't leave, causing damage as they do so?

When I found that damaged washing machine gasket, I went online, searched through some videos, and found one that shows exactly how to replace the gasket for my particular machine. I ordered the part, and it arrived within 5 days. I fitted it and our problem was solved.

It didn't cost a lot of money, and the repair was far cheaper than a new drum, or a new washing machine, and far cheaper than getting an engineer out to repair it.

So where is God asking us to take the lid off of our lives – the one we like to keep firmly sealed so nobody sees the delicate parts of our emotional wellbeing and inner-workings? And if we identify what is not working correctly, do we allow skilled people to help us? Or God?

The encouraging thing about living a life with God in it is that He's really gentle in fixing us and helping us work at our optimum level.

God made you, and He made me. And He did so by the work of His own hand!

Psalm 139 v 13-14 tells us that He made us, and He knows us. So, He knows how you are made and how you are designed.

> *For you formed my inward parts; you knitted me together in my mother's womb. I praise you, for I am fearfully and wonderfully made. Wonderful are your works; my soul knows it very well. (English Standard Version)*

There are always going to be things that seek to distort the protective seals of our lives, and seek to create damage, and distance, between us and God.

Will you trust God, and let Him take a proper look inside your heart and mind and replace, repair, and make right what He sees?

He truly is a good God, and He hand made you, so already knows all about you. Will you trust Him?

Just a thought…

8. Plastic Bottles, Sheep and the Holy Spirit

A really good friend of mine was preaching about sheep, and how we are so very much like them, and why the Bible regularly uses sheep as an analogy for us as Christians. He was talking about some really great experiences he'd had, and it got me thinking about sheep – and us.

I remembered some milkshake that we had one time when I saw the empty plastic bottles waiting to be recycled.

And, while I haven't got a rug made from sheepskin, or a fleece blanket made from wool, I do have a modern fleece jacket, and fleece jackets can easily be made from recycled plastic bottles, as much as they can be made from wool.

All of that got me thinking about how things can be recycled and reused.

Perhaps you're allowing yourself to define 'you' by a lack of money, or by the fact you don't feel good enough, or by whether or not you pray long enough or frequently enough. But those negative thoughts can build up and impact how we think God sees us.

When we walk in step with God; when we pursue Him, the Holy Spirit works in us and growth in the Fruit of the Spirit naturally occurs. It spontaneously happens out of a relationship with God, as my Study Bible articulated well.

If we picture ourselves as sheep, we come to understand that sheep don't have to work hard themselves in order to create fleece. That's just what happens. It isn't a conscious effort to grow wool! They simply munch on grass, and the fleece grows. It's the same with the Fruit of the Spirit. We seek to grow closer to God and it happens within us.

The discarded plastic bottle is rubbish to us when we've used its contents. And while it may be no good to us at that point, when it's refined properly – by someone who knows what to do with it – it becomes valuable once again. It never actually loses its value.

Perhaps you're allowing the difficult times you've experienced, as well as some of those poor personal choices, to define how you think, and believe, God sees you. But God loves you. And, just like the sheep He loves, we only need to follow the sound of His voice and wait, and trust, that He will come to help us.

And, just like those discarded plastic bottles, you aren't rubbish either.

So, let's let the Shepherd come close to us and trust that His plans are to care for us and to prosper us.

Just a thought…

9. Christmas Trees and Good Wrestles

Jo was preparing for a week away on a residential training course. With Christmas drawing ever closer, we decided to get a little wild and get the Christmas tree and lights up and twinkling a little earlier than usual!

So, one free evening, we got every Christmas decoration we owned set up and plugged in! We even found a few more. I firmly believe there is no such thing as too many lights!

We looked at our Christmas tree, however, and unanimously decided that it really was rather small and pathetic! And so began our quest for a real Christmas Tree that was, not to put too fine a point on it, big enough to see without a magnifying glass and plenty of time searching.

So, after what felt like many weeks and months (probably just 2 hours), and thousands of shops (probably just 5), we finally found the perfect tree for our home. Only, it was stuck in a metal cage, in the entrance to a busy supermarket, and I was with a shop assistant who looked like he'd rather have been, well, anywhere else.

I was on my own! My wife describes me as having the tenacity of a Yorkshire Terrier. That tree agreed.

To start with I was fairly gentle, but as difficulty led to frustration and irritation, I got ever more aggressive ripping the trees in my way to one side, until I had my prize in the "Great Tree Quest of 2020".

As with most family trips of this nature, loading it in the car, with 5 people already in it, was the greater challenge. You can picture heads contorted to one side and hands steadying the tree to stop it from smashing against a window or a face.

Once we finally got it home, a new challenge emerged. We had a Christmas tree base for a very large tree. Our new tree was bigger than the base. In one final flurry, and wielding my saw, I trimmed the base until it would fit in to our Christmas tree base.

We added the lights we had in our home plus some more we had purchased to go with it.

Where are you wrestling with something that is worth wrestling with?

Sometimes, it's really good to keep wrestling for the prize we're aiming for. Sure, we need to recognise when to move on to the next tree, but sometimes we just need to roll our sleeves, up, take a deep breath, and get stuck in!

Where can you feel God urging you to keep wrestling?

Keep going!

Our tree was worth the fight. It warmed our room, our home, and our street. Your wrestle may just warm the heart of someone who had lost hope when they see your determination to keep going.

Just a thought…

10. The God Connection – Dial Up or High Speed Broadband

Our next-door neighbour had a problem with the main electrical feed coming into their home. It came in from the street in front of our houses, then branched off to each home. In order to repair the issue with their mains cable, we had to have our power turned off too.

The workmen who turned up were quick, friendly, and professional. The problem, which they told us could have proved fatal for our neighbours if left unattended, was put right; they replaced the thin, seemingly unimportant earthing cable that protected the house and occupants from surges in electricity.

This reminded me of a similar issue we'd had, in a previous home, with our Radio Broadband signal. Well, 'similar' maybe a bit of a stretch!

We lived in an area where landlines for telephones and the internet lines simply did not exist. We were simply too far away from the nearest junction box which meant the signal couldn't travel far all the way to our little village.

A local company had established a Radio Broadband network to meet the need for high speed, reliable internet, using satellite dishes, and repeater stations to bounce an internet signal all over the village, and up the mountain we lived to ever more remote dwellings.

Occasionally they used actual cables to push the signal even further, using farmers' fields and burying the cables far enough down to keep them safe.

One day our internet signal suddenly stopped. Have you ever noticed that things never break when it is convenient?!?

I called up the people who supplied our internet signal, who conducted multiple diagnostic tests only to conclude that it was a problem at our end. I knew that it wasn't us, so kept pushing them to resolve the issue.

Eventually, out of frustration, they checked those very few places where cable was used. And found that some sheep had been munching on the cable that had, somehow, been brought up to the surface.

They hadn't chewed all the way through – just enough so that a diagnostic test could get a return, but not enough for any internet to flow through.

It didn't take them long to replace the cable and deliver a sheepish apology to us. But the cable had been replaced, and all was good again!

All of that made me wonder about those connections we have in our relationship with God, and I wondered what a diagnostic test might pick up our own hard lines to God.

Perhaps it might detect that prayer which you said to God yesterday, when everything else you had tried failed. Perhaps it would pick up that Bible study you attended last week, where you spent the entire time with your phone inside the biggest Bible you could find, catching up on those urgent work emails you forgot to reply to.

The diagnostic test may well find that there is indeed a connection between you and God. But is it a good signal? Or is it one that is simply strong enough for a diagnostic test to get a return from, but not good enough to really hear from God?

Perhaps you keep it slightly broken, so you can get on with your life a little more easily?

Putting this another way, is there a connection you have with God which needs some urgent repair work?

Just like the issue with the cables supplying our neighbours with their electricity, or the cables supplying our internet, no matter how bad the problem is, when we identify it, God can repair it. No matter how bad it was won't matter once it has been repaired.

Let God run some diagnostics as you listen to the Holy Spirit. Or perhaps you could run your own – where do you know you are not listening to God, or perhaps are preventing yourself from hearing God's voice?

Just a thought…

11. Car Wheels and Realignments

As I was sitting in a church service, where they were talking about cars and lights – and how God lights the next part of the road we're journeying along – it made me think about our own car, and how we recently had to get the wheels realigned.

With the many rather deep, swimming pools we regularly drive through – described as potholes by the people who maintain our road network – those wheels on our car were soon out of alignment.

To the naked eye, those 4 wheels looked as though they were all going in exactly the same direction. However, they really were not and, using some lasers, it was easy to see exactly how far out those wheels had all become. They were certainly not travelling in exactly the same direction any longer. They were, each of them, pointing their own way!

As you drive a car along the road, and hit a bump, the rods which keep those wheels pointing in the same direction, absorb some of that 'bump' and that forces them out of alignment one bump at a time.

The longer you leave it, and the more bumps you hit, or the harder you hit them, the worse that alignment gets, and the more pronounced the problem presents itself to the driver through the steering wheel.

It decreases fuel economy at best, and ruins tyres very rapidly. If it gets really bad it makes your car unstable and, in wet conditions, can make it very dangerous as the 4 wheels each try and fight with each other for control. This is never good!

Once a mechanic had corrected the tracking of those 4 wheels, it was immediately noticeable – when driving away – what a difference it had made as the steering felt significantly lighter than before, and the car no longer tried to pull to one side as you drove along the road. When it rained you no longer found yourself clinging onto the steering wheel when driving along at high speed.

And all this talk of cars made me think about how important it is to be regularly realigned with God. I'd often quoted this, and mentioned it at various times, but I'd never really considered the importance of doing so.

As you drive a car, lots of smaller bumps can create equal damage to your tracking, as much as hitting a few larger potholes. The real danger is that those smaller little bumps are harder to spot as they affect the tracking of a car much less, so we're less able to spot that steering wheel becoming less and less positive about its job!

And our relationship with God is exactly the same. Sure, we can hit a few big holes in the road, and we can feel that distance between us and God. But, it's the smaller bumps that can create the real damage – making a personal phone call from work without permission; rushing through a traffic light even though we know it just turned red; claiming for expenses and adding a few miles to the figures; claiming for overtime and rounding all those hours we worked up just a little bit.

All of those 'little things' add up and create distance between us and God. Some of them are downright dangerous, and others are actually illegal!

To God, they are one and the same because they all put a little more distance between us and God.

So, when did you last realign yourself to God? When did you last confess all those things you knew were wrong? When did you last spend time just listening to the voice of His Holy Spirit to ensure you're walking the path God actually wants you to walk?

Just a thought...

12. Cardboard Cut Outs And Trying Again

One of the things that we've learned to do as a family is to be adaptable, and flexible, when filming for the BerryBunch. One of our regular broadcasts is Art Time, which forms part of Little Blessings Online. And we concluded that Art Time would look best if we could hold a camera directly above the artwork being worked on. However, short of Velcro ties and string, we struggled to find a way of doing this well, and repeatedly.

Initially, we used a webcam that we secured, albeit badly but securely. But this really wasn't especially ideal!

As we developed how we worked with our recording we started using a mobile phone to film instead. And we really didn't want to secure a personal mobile phone, several feet above a hard surface, just with pieces of string and some hope! Frustratingly, the very things we were using to fasten the phone in place also prevented us from being able to use the screen on the phone, which we needed to change things like the focus and the all-important white balance.

And then, in a flash of brain like things and inspiration, I came up with a solution that was more Blue Peter than high end filming equipment!

I took a piece of cardboard, cut it, and shaped it into a sort of triangle like shape, with a flat base. I created holes in it for the lens of a mobile phone to see through, and set it on the boom arm of a microphone stand that we'd made horizontal. And our adjustable, reusable, mobile phone cradle was born.

My first version utterly failed, so that went in the bin. The second version was even worse. But, by my third attempt, I'd got it! With a few more Andy B-type flares of creativity we had what we needed to recreate the same scene to film Art Time, whenever we needed to.

With the first version, it nearly worked, but it was a bit too squashed and flat, and I couldn't get to the mobile phone screen when I'd finished. With version 2 I'd made the refinements I needed to retain access with the phones screen, but I ended up with a bigger mess of cardboard cut badly, and sticky tape everywhere. By version 3, I'd made all the additional refinements, even making it future proof, by making access holes sufficiently larger for a range of possible mobile phones.

What I ended up doing with a piece of cardboard, some sticky tape and a pair of scissors got me wondering about life, and those times when we've given up too quickly. Or perhaps, after we had one quick success, and a seemingly endless run of failures soon after, we just give up getting back up and trying again.

My 3rd attempt doesn't exactly look pretty! But, it functions well and has lasted well over a year so far. It isn't pretty, but it is functional. Perhaps I can create a 4th version and cover it with some coloured paper. Either way I'm pretty chuffed with my efforts.

So, where is God wanting you to try again at something? Where do you feel God urging you to have another go at something?

I built a stand for my computer monitor because I could never get it in the right place. With some confidence gained by my mobile phone cradle, I got some pieces of wood, screwed them together into a decking of sorts, and now I have the monitor at the perfect height for my eyes, chair, and desk.

I wonder how often we simply keep struggling along, without even wondering if we could fix the thing we're struggling with.

So, where does God want you to trust Him and try again? Where does He want you to take something you've learned, and used, but make it even better?

Just a thought…

13. Rice Maker Handles

We love rice in our home, and we've been using a microwave rice maker for years! Our particular model of microwave maker has a helpful little red handle on top of the lid, that lets you pick up the lid without scalding yourself. Always good!

But this little red handle kept coming off fairly frequently as we used it. We had to make a decision: do we glue it back on – which had its own obvious issues – or leave it off and simply pop it in a drawer until we can work out what to do with it?

When we moved into a new house we were left a microwave by the owner to make use of. But this microwave must have been designed for use by baby hobbits because it was really small! Our rice maker would fit inside, but only just, and never with that little red handle.

This got me thinking two things.

The first is that nothing going on in our lives is ever either wasted, or beyond redemption by God, no matter how low or broken we feel. We're always useful for God's plans, and our feelings about ourselves make no difference. God is after our hearts, not our abilities or successes.

The second thing that it got me thinking is about those things we hang onto; that we cling onto. They make us feel safe, but God longs for us to let go in order to give us something far more wholesome and beneficial for us.

Our microwave rice maker is great. The replacement microwave we've been given to us works wonderfully, even if it is super tiny. But that little red handle, as helpful as it has been in the past, is no longer of any use and needs removing and casting to one side. It simply has no use any longer.

So, where in your life have you got similarly pointless little red handles that used to look great once upon a time; that used to be super helpful, but are now just a hindrance. Or perhaps, they're all we have left of a broken tea pot we smashed and lost years ago. The only thing left to do is throw that handle away, and let God put something much more useful in your hand for you to hold onto.

Just a thought…

14. Stripey Fabric and Usefulness

In our very first home Jo and I were given a settee that somebody no longer wanted. We were living in a police house, which was great – because it was huge. But, as newlyweds, we had little money and certainly no furniture. That second-hand settee was a very welcome addition and a huge improvement from sitting on the floor!

However, it wasn't very nice to look at due its age and how much it had been used over the years. So, we thought about covering it with something to brighten it up a little. And while we couldn't afford to buy any fabric, I did have a working mobile phone which we could sell – to pay for some fabric to cover that settee.

I sold it to a local man who worked as a gritter driver for the council trucks. He was super happy that he got a replacement phone, and we were super happy that we'd got enough money to go out and buy some fabric.

We walked into our local town centre, found a wonderfully stocked, and old fashioned fabric shop where were found a roll of stripey red fabric that caught our eye.

At this point in time, that fabric has reached more than 25 years of age and is still going strong! It was a high quality fabric when we used up every last penny from the sale of my mobile phone to buy it.

That quality has shown itself over the years because we've used it all over many homes we've lived in, for a whole host of reasons.

We've used it to cover internal glass doors. We've used it in place of curtains or rolled up on the floor to stop drafts. We've used it to create sounds barriers for our home filming studio. And, yes, we've even used it to cover settees!

For our family, this cloth has developed its own special meaning because it's something that Jo and I invested in, nearly a quarter of a century ago – and it's still going strong!

With all of that 'usefulness' the fabric is certainly not in its original condition anymore – it has rips and holes where it has been hung on screws, or on curtain poles, or on the backs of doors. As the ends of each strip of fabric got tatty and shredded from use, we even added hems to try and tidy the ends up.

It now has numerous holes, rips, and tears. They each tell something of our story, some of which we still remember fondly.

In our lives there are regular incidents, and moments, that can stir up our hearts and minds, taking us back to memories from our past, whether they be good or bad memories.

If we ever tried to sell our stripey red fabric, I might be able to sell it as "vintage", but it will never be in "mint condition", ever again. But it still holds great value for us because of those memories it stirs up in us.

Usefulness is a very relative term in a throwaway society. We don't use the fabric to cover a settee anymore, but we do use it for many other things, and it looks to remain useful to us for many years to come.

Wherever you are in your relationship with God – if you feel that you've been useful in the past but are not useful any longer – please do know that you are always useful to God!

This fabric – which we have kept these past two and a half decades – reminds me of the fact that we never go past being useful to God, because, with God, we can never be beyond His use. He is after willing hearts, not skilled hands or the ability to maintain a healthy bank balance.

Those many holes, and rips, and marks make the fabric look damaged. But they also tell a story – of a life lived. And the wounds and marks on your life can remind you, and others too, that you have also made an impact on the world.

So, no matter how you've lived your life, or what may have happened to you – either because of you, or against your will – God can, and will, be able to use you, whoever you are, wherever you are, because you are always worth it to God.

Just a thought…

15. Remote Controlled Alarm Clocks and The Holy Spirit

I found myself with a faithful alarm clock no longer able to tell the time. It had been working faithfully for some 17 years but, just a few days earlier, it stopped working. The Radio Control function had stopped working, so it simply wasn't communicating properly, and no longer knew what the time was. Not great for an alarm clock!

When we woke up one morning my clock was showing the wrong time. Jo was telling me that it was time to leave for church, but my clock was telling me something quite different when I looked at it.

It had once had some really useful functions – which had also stopped working. For example, there was a dial on the side which you could turn in order to focus the image it projected on to your bedroom ceiling. For a man who wears glasses, this was just brilliant! But it had taken to only showing part of the time, leaving you guessing the rest. Not overly helpful when you're bleary eyed at 3am!

And, while I can live without seeing a large projected time on my bedroom ceiling, I can't live with an alarm clock that can't tell the time, so it was duly dispatched to the great alarm clock heaven we affectionally call the bin!

However, the sadness of losing my much loved alarm clock was soon tempered by the greater excitement of being able to buy a new one! And mine looks funky, modern, and even has a cockerel for its alarm sound. The running water alarm sound just makes me want the toilet – that's just cruel – but I love it!

This got me wondering about our relationships with God. Because, with God, sometimes it feels a bit like we're badly working the gears on a car with a manual gear box (a stick shift).

If we get it wrong, we usually end up with a horrible grinding noise, because elements of the gear system in the car are simply not meshing together properly. They are not working together and that lack of meshing, or synchronisation, is what causes people to stop and stare at what we're doing while your car makes screaming, and grinding, noises.

The Holy Spirit helps us to stay in tune with God and to walk in time with Him.

Another way of saying this is that the Holy Spirit helps us to be reconciled to God, or to mesh with Him – just like the synchromesh gearbox was designed to work. This alignment of us to God is what the Holy Spirit does so very well for us; every day we are moving towards God, and away from God, and back again. Over the course of a single day, much like the signal we rely upon for our internet, it can get all out of alignment, needing to be synchronised once again.

If our internet is struggling, we turn off the router and then turn it back on again, and that fixes the problem. It allows the signal being fed to our home the opportunity to sort itself out and get synchronised again, so our computer can see what it needs to.

In our cars, we slow down that gear change and try again. Or perhaps just buy an automatic car next time to take the gear change out of the equation!

And, in our relationships with God, it simply involves stopping what we're doing, at regular intervals, in order to listen to Him. Once we've established where God is again, we can adjust our gait to be in step with Him once more.

I could have kept my alarm clock for posterity because it had given service for a long time. But when it could no longer carry out the one thing I needed it to do and wasn't able to be repaired – or resynchronised – it simply needed to be disposed of.

To reconcile ourselves with God, all we need to do is take moments to stop and pause and hush. We don't throw away the relationship, because it can always be reconciled once again.

Just a thought…

16. Punctures, Goals and Rolling with Resistance

We love riding our mountain bikes together as husband and wife, but one ride was a little more eventful than usual. Or perhaps I should say that it was less eventful than usual because I experienced a pretty bad puncture which brought our ride to a rather undramatic stop!

All my wife Jo, and I, wanted to do was simply get out of the house, go for that mountain bike ride together, and get back home again so we could get on with the many other things that needed doing that day.

We even managed to meet up with our oldest son, who was out on a cross-country run. We were having a really enjoyable time together. And then my puncture happened.

Up to that point, we had thought that we could have caught up with our son again, after he had blasted past us as were puffing our way up a steep hill.

At one point we managed to work out that he was running at around 6 miles per hour, and we were cycling at around 6 miles per hour. So, we knew, if we pushed a little harder, that we might be able to catch up with him again, even get past him, and perhaps beat him home.

But it was at that exact point, just as we had decided to really push on hard to catch up and overtake him, that the puncture happened – it stopped us reaching our goal. And we'd literally just spotted him ahead of us, just in reach.

So often in life we have goals that we're trying to reach and accomplish. We decide, and even believe, that "we're gonna do this."

We had planned to go for a mountain bike ride – and we did. We were nearly keeping up with our firstborn son, who was much fitter than we were. And we were doing that too, for a while.

Having goals can be great. Goals can be great fun and they can inspire and motivate us to try things, or focus on getting things done that we otherwise might not ever even have tried to accomplish.

On the other hand, some goals we're trying to reach can end up demotivating us from ever trying again.

I always carry a portable bicycle pump. I always carry the tools I need for the vast majority of breakdowns that might occur while cycling. I even have the knowledge to fix a puncture when away from home. But being prepared doesn't always prevent us from failing to meet our goals, because life happens and throws things at us that no matter of preparedness can affect!

It can be quite frustrating when our plans don't work out as we had hoped, even when we have done everything in our power to ensure we can follow through with them.

On that occasion, no matter how prepared we might have been, we had to stop to resolve the issue at hand and our goal disappeared into the distance, literally!

The phrase 'every cloud has a silver lining' came to mind that day.

While we didn't have any plans to stop where we did, and while beating Steven home would have been a fantastic achievement, Jo and I were forced to stop in an utterly idyllic spot in the countryside near our home.

We had a lovely chat together while I fixed the puncture, and we enjoyed that private moment together, that we hadn't planned for and couldn't have scripted even if we'd wanted to.

Our unplanned stop turned out well for us because of that time we got to spend together on that beautifully, uncharacteristically warm, British summer day.

So, when your goals don't work out as planned, try and roll with the resistance. 'Tuck and roll' is a great skill to learn – being adaptable is a great way of being able to make the most of the situations we find ourselves in, no matter what happens.

And, when things go awry, don't panic! It might be that God had something better planned the whole time anyway, and our frustration can become a blessing when we get out of the way of ourselves and God's plans for our life.

Just a thought…

17. Tape Measures and Limits

I don't know how knowledgeable you are with DIY tools, but some tape measures have a special device that is super helpful in stopping the tape measure whizzing back into itself. This can lead to causing damage to your finger, and to your tape measure – it's an addition I always look for when I have to replace a tape measure. It's essentially a brake you can apply with your thumb.

I had found myself having to buy a new tape measure, after our older one had stopped working anymore, and after that thumb-brake had failed once too often leading to a little blood loss from my finger!

This new tape measure had an extra feature I liked because, in very obvious lettering, they'd printed the word STOP near the very end of the tape measure.

You presume that this was because, if you pull the tape measure past that STOP sign, you could break it. In this case, STOP marked the end of the usable part, beyond which it simply wasn't designed to be pulled any further!

Unfortunately, and I'm sure you can guess where I'm going with this, somebody pulled that tape measure too far, and it became useless. My brand-new tape measure was broken and destined for the bin before I'd even managed to yet use it!

At this point in my story, we had a tape measure that extended across the entire garden and wouldn't retract, at all! On the plus side, though, I got to go to a hardware shop and search for another tape measure, which is always a pleasant experience!

Some things can be repaired, and some things really can't. My brand-new tape measure was one of the latter – it was beyond repair and so went in the bin as I couldn't come up with many reasons to have a permanently outstretched, 5-metre-long tape measure.

But that memory makes me wonder about those red STOP signs that we see in life – those times when we see the word STOP in giant red letters, warning us not to keep going, but we choose to ignore it and carry on doing what we were doing anyway. As with my shiny tape measure, we just end up breaking something, possibly even ourselves.

It's a little like a set of traffic lights – red lights, at traffic junctions and intersections – that tell us that we need to stop, so we don't rush into danger. We ignore those signs at our peril.

Maybe it is simply a sign on your tape measure that you pull to far, breaking it. It's fairly easy to replace a tape measure!

But some of those STOP signs that we ignore create damage that can't be so quickly sorted out. Perhaps we wonder, "Well, how bad could it really be if I carry on down this particular path, or doing that particular thing?"

So, where is there a STOP sign in your life, that you know God is asking you to see and obey, but you know you've been ignoring so far?

Or, perhaps, where is God asking you to STOP something in your life before you end up going too far and breaking something, or perhaps even someone – including yourself?

In life there are STOP signs that are designed to prevent us from carrying on into danger. And, just because we can go past something, it doesn't mean to say we should!

Perhaps that flashing red light on the dashboard of your life is a warning light that really needs some attention.

Just a thought…

18. Projection, Reality and Giant Spiders

Picture, if you will, a giant spider. This may be something you didn't wish to do, but I bet you're doing it now .

Anyway, you're here now, so picture a giant spider.

Now British spiders are fairly mild in size when compared to some of the spiders you can find in other countries.

In the UK, I'd describe a large spider as something up to perhaps 5 inches across (from the ends of its legs). At that size, it'd be what I would define as large. Something that size would certainly both surprise and shock me.

One morning, Jo and I were sitting in the bed having a relaxed start to the day.

We were having a pleasant conversation about life and slowly supping away at our favourite early morning brew, before moving on into the day.

It was in this rather relaxed state that I then spotted it on the wall, right behind my wife's head. It was the shadow of a spider – some 10 centimetres across. This was in my 5 worst case scenarios for a spider!

I was certainly surprised and, being the dutiful husband, I immediately jumped into action as my wife's superhero, yanking her forwards and away from that giant spider, which I envisaged threatening to cause permanent harm to my much beloved wife at any moment.

Having jumped out of bed and wondering "what the heck is this monstrous nightmare in our home, and from whence did it come!?!" we looked, and I could not find this thing no matter how hard I looked.

Exactly how do you lose a spider that big? I know spiders can be quick, but they're not that quick!

So, why couldn't I find this monstrous, steel-toe-capped-boot-wearing, tattooed, piercing-touting beast anywhere. It wasn't on Jo.

It wasn't on the bed, on the wall, under the bed, on or either of our bedside tables. It really wasn't anywhere to be found!

I began wondering how something that huge could simply disappear. I started to even question my own sanity. I had recently been watching the Lord of the Rings after all, and Shelob – the giant spider in the last book – is one you don't quickly forget!

It was at this point that I noticed this micro sized spider that was perhaps just half a millimetre across – like the width of a grain of rice.

On closer inspection, it appeared that this particular arachnid seemed to have a rather dark sense of humour, because it was having a little play with us, by walking across some tiny LED lights that we had put around the top of our bed frame, projecting its image onto the wall behind Jo's head, some 10 centimetres across.

This situation with the spider and its shadow got me thinking about those issues in our lives where we're seeing something that simply isn't what we think it is, because we're seeing the projected image, and not the real thing

The devil loves projecting images where we can see them; he revels in getting us to see problems and situations that are insurmountable and impossibly bigger than us.

At best his goal is to simply force us to only do good things for people, rather than God things.

Much like David and Goliath, however, the harder they come, the harder they fall, because big doesn't equate to scary when you know who has your back, like David did knowing Goliath had already been defeated in his mind.

All he had to do was turn up and do as he was told by God!

Would I have had the same reaction to that new-born, baby-hobbit-sized spider if I'd first seen it for real, sitting on a light, laughing at us in all its miniature glory? Of course not!

And so it is with the projected fear that the devil loves to illuminate in front of us, in fuzzy 4K quality just big enough to appear believable.

So, let's have the last laugh and take a good, long look at the truth. Let's shine a light on the truth and let that truth set us free!

Just a thought…

19. James, Conviction and Liberation

James Chapter 1 v 5-8.

> *If any of you lacks wisdom, let him ask God, who gives generously to all without reproach, and it will be given him. But let him ask in faith, with no doubting, for the one who doubts is like a wave of the sea that is driven and tossed by the wind. For that person must not suppose that he will receive anything from the Lord; he is a double-minded man, unstable in all his ways. (English Standard Version)*

Have you ever tried to quietly move around the bedroom in the deepest dark of the night, when you're desperate for the toilet, but are also trying to be super quiet so that you don't wake anybody else up? And have you ever decided against using a torch (flashlight) to light your path?

It's usually as you finally near your goal that you get a bit too confident, stub your toe, and cry out, and your efforts backfire badly as the entire household is woken up to investigate who is being violently murdered in your bedroom, only to find it was just you stubbing your toe on the end of the bed.

If you were sensible, you'd have used a torch, but you didn't. So now, instead, you have a bruised ego, as well as a bruised toe that isn't even showing signs of your near-death experience.

For me, James is that torch that we need in our daily lives. His words create a gentler approach to moving through life. They are the torch in the darkness that prevents stubbed toes.

We had been working on our family ministry, The BerryBunch, for more than a year, building it up from literally nothing – just a few chats in our garden and a vague idea of what we hoped to achieve. And yet I constantly found myself wondering whether this really was what God wanted me to do with my time, or with our time as a family.

I was led to read that passage from James, and those verses, coupled with the conviction of the Holy Spirit, and a wife who is happy to speak righteous truth into my life, helped me with something of a slap to the back of my head to help me wake up!

I was being double minded, because if I did something, I'd look for a get-out in case things went wrong. And if things went well, I'd write it off as a fluke.

I wasn't committing to what we had confirmed God was asking us to do, and it was exhausting me!

While it's never good to rush into anything, it's even worse, I think, if you know what you should do, but don't do it. Being uncertain is one thing. But knowledge, coupled with ignorance, is just exhausting, as it eats away at our very existence!

My double mindedness had led me to wonder "Where has God gone?" And yet, of course, if we are double minded, then we are upsetting the Holy Spirit. And that will make us feel distant from God.

So, where are you being double minded?

Where has God given you clear instructions on what to do, but you've ignored Him? Perhaps you're waiting for that writing to appear in the sky that confirms the 17 random messages from God you've already had?

Or, where are you doing something, but not giving your whole self to it? You're just trying to float on the surface and not doing anything to actually 'action' what you're doing.

Let's do all we can to ensure that we're walking in faith, trusting God, and walking righteously, without feeling the need to wait until the resources and end results are already in place, but trusting God for the next step, and just getting on with the current step.

And, if God has given you something to do, and you know what that is, don't be double minded about it, but jump in with both feet and trust that God will provide all you need as you walk forwards.

Just a thought…

20. Samuel, David and Uncertainty

While preparing to film an episode of one of our regular broadcasts – Endurance – I was looking through 1 Samuel, chapter 16 and reading about how Samuel was asked – by God – to choose the next King.

As it goes, Jesse was asked by the prophet Samuel to present his sons, who dutifully turned out, in order to be paraded in front of this man of God.

Basically, Samuel was to walk up and down in front of Jesse's sons, inspect each one, and ask God if that particular son was the right man to be King or not. And God would say 'yes' or 'no'. Simples!

But as Samuel is checking each of those sons, He hears the same repeated words from God: *"The Lord has not chosen these."* So, Samuel asks Jesse: *"Are all your sons here?"* And Jesse replies: *"There remains yet the youngest, but behold, he is keeping the sheep."* So, Samuel tells Jesse to *"Send and get him, for we will not sit down till he comes here."*

As Samuel looked at Jesse's sons, from his perspective as he moved along that line, it was clear that the sons started off looking like the perfect candidates for the job.

They were tall.

They were big.

They were rugged.

They looked kingly!

But, as we so often see, God has a very different idea of who is best to serve Him in a particular way, because God is God. And God desires willing hearts, not shredded muscles.

So, where are you looking at a situation and saying, "Well, I think God wants me to do *this*, but it doesn't quite look like that from what I'm seeing right now"?

Of course, God saw those rugged looking, muscular sons of Jesse, but he also saw their hearts and knew that they weren't right for what He had planned.

And yes, of course God saw how small David was in comparison to his brothers. But, as we learn later David was *"a man after God's own heart"*, and if you're gonna choose a King, you want to choose the man who has a heart that chases after God, not the man who could beat everybody else in an arm wrestle or make the young women swoon!

Far too many people talk about a greater need for common sense in our world and in the church. But, in God's kingdom at least, common sense is about as useful as a chocolate fireguard, because what God desires is people who are willing to exercise God-Sense, not common sense.

We don't need people who are happy to exercise common sense – human wisdom based on experience. Who determines what common sense is anyway?! It's very relative and changes with time.

What we really need are people who can take a few pebbles to a fight with a giant knowing they can't lose, despite everybody telling them they're just being stupid.

What we really need are men of faith like Noah, who can endure the mocking and name calling and cruelty, to obey God and build a boat in the middle of a desert for the rain that is nowhere in sight.

David and Noah were not common sense men. They were God-Sense men!

Knowing our calling doesn't give us licence to go charging along, like a bull with hurt feelings.

Instead, we should walk forwards Biblically, prayerfully, and wisely – stepping forwards into the void before us and doing so with the boldness that can only come by being certain of who we are in God, and who God is in us!

Just a thought…

21. David, Benaiah, Goliath and Respect

I had taken some time out to read my Bible. I was reading a plan that led me to take a good look at King David, and to Samuel chapter 17: David and Goliath.

This account has been made into all manner of things, from assemblies to Sunday School Lessons to a myriad of Sermons, and it's been interwoven into a hundred books or more. And yet David fighting Goliath is just one little verse in the middle of the other 58 verses that make up 1 Samul chapter 17.

My favourite Bible character is a man named Benaiah, who went on to become King David's bodyguard. The same boy who slayed Goliath and became King had a rather unique skill set in one of his personal bodyguards, and a couple of rather relevant shared experiences.

David and Benaiah had both killed lions. And they had both killed giants.

David had killed a lion to protect his father's sheep. Benaiah had gone one better and chased a lion into a pit, on a snowy day, and killed it; Benaiah's giant hadn't been quite as imposing as Goliath, but a giant is a giant – and killing one is simply not something that you do every day.

David killing Goliath is an amazing little verse! But even more striking to me than what happened on the battlefield is what had taken place off the battlefield before David ever stepped in front of Goliath. Because David had already slayed his nemesis before picking up those smooth stones and setting out for the front line.

David trusted that no matter what he would face, if he was doing it under God's direction, he could not fail! If you know God is bigger than anything you could ever face, what could you ever face that was bigger than God?

What Goliaths are you facing or seeing in your immediate future? Without belittling those struggles ahead, if you know God is bigger than anything you could ever face, as with the small shepherd – David – what do you have to worry about?

The things we fear have a tendency to grow in size and severity when we focus on them for too long. When we look too closely and focus on the problem, rather than the Problem-Solver, we give those fears permission to grow inside our hearts and minds. Defeat is already assured against us!

But, when we remember who it is that we have behind us – God – then defeat is already assured, but in our favour!

When we are certain that God is bigger than any problem we could ever face, what's the problem?

We can name it unemployment, or cancer, conviction from a crime, or just a nasty bully in our office or workplace. When we know who God really is, we can enter the battlefield with victory assured: the end of the battle rarely resembles what we assumed it would look like. However, with God, we can never lose in His eyes, and that's what really matters!

David had already taken on and defeated Goliath – in his mind – before ever stepping on to the battlefield. He knew that he couldn't fail because he was under God's orders.

So, let's step forward boldly for God, just like David did, all while knowing that if God is calling us forwards to take on something we fear, we can do so knowing He already has our back, and our side, and our front.

With God, the victory is assured, because it has already been fought and won!

Just a thought…

22. Helping Others Can Be Easy!

I was taking the opportunity to drive my wife, Jo, to work one day. It's a great way for us to spend a little extra time together during the working day. I don't mind the driving; Jo gets a rest – it's a win-win, because the cost is offset by the extra time I get with my best friend!

The sacrifice for me was, perhaps, 90 minutes of my time, twice in a day, and, as a former Heavy Goods Vehicle driver (properly big trucks!), who was used to doing 4 ½ hours driving without a break, twice a day, a couple of drives – at 90 minutes each – wasn't even a full morning's work or a single drive in my driver's seat!

Yes, it was a sacrifice. I took time when I could have been doing other things, but it was a worthwhile sacrifice, because the reward was time with my beautiful wife – the one who I can always rely upon to laugh at my jokes. And, as an added bonus, it meant I could also pop into a Post Office, which was quite a distance from our home. And I got to shop at a bigger supermarket for some foodstuffs we otherwise struggled to obtain.

So, where is God prompting you to help somebody else?

It can be really easy, simple, and straightforward to help others, and often at very little personal cost. It might be just a few hours of your time when you've got plenty of time to spare.

Helping others makes us feel better, although if you're clearing the garden of someone who needs that sort of help, your back may not thank you in the evening. But helping others doesn't have to be complicated, or costly, or hard!

I learned at a Business Resourcing event many years ago that the only thing we each have which is freely available to give away is our time.

Our time really is our own and we truly can choose what to do with it. It is, literally, the only thing we all have that we can choose how to spend.

Sure, we may choose to go to work to earn money to buy food and keep a roof over our heads. We may even be forced to serve time in a prison. But no matter what situation we find ourselves in, we can still choose how to spend our time, even if that choice is limited more to whether we smile at others or not. We still have a choice.

So, what is God asking you to do to help somebody else today?

Who is God asking you to help tomorrow?

It might be as simple as giving someone a lift or sending an email to somebody to brighten their day with a favourite BerryBunch video or Post (a free suggestion!).

Perhaps it's a phone call you've been putting off for some time, because you don't know if your offering of your time or skill set will be good enough.

It might be as simple as smiling at the checkout assistant after a grumpy customer has just stormed off leaving chaos in their wake.

Whatever God is asking you to do is very worth your time, because you cannot know the end result of your one action of kindness towards somebody else.

I've let people merge in front of me on the road when everybody is at their busiest, and I have sometimes been pleased to see that person let somebody else in, and so on. Was that me? Perhaps, but it was worth it either way.

Finally, we shouldn't seek to help others just so we can be assured of receiving their help in return in the future. That approach can easily lead to bitterness and resentment building up in us when that other person either cannot, or will not, render us the assistance we feel we are owed.

In the same way that we should give our money freely towards the work of God, we should also freely give our time. In fact, your 'tithing' may well be your time.

Just a thought…

23. God's Rhythms, and Busy Days

Once upon a time I managed to take heed of my own, frequently spoken advice – about the importance of taking moments to hush and pause before God, especially when the day ahead looks overly crammed full, with far too much work, impossible deadlines, and not enough time to accomplish it all.

Those are the days when taking some time out before you dive in becomes even more important – no matter how counterintuitive that might appear a first.

This isn't some sort of secret formula or hack that enables us to squeeze even more out of our capability, to help us accomplish more than we should be able to do humanly. It is, however, about doing all that God is asking us to do so we can achieve everything God sets out for us to do – when we walk with Him at His pace, in His rhythm, and at His direction.

The problem, as ever, is knowing what God is asking us to do, over the many good, or must-be-done things that we assume we must be doing.

Isaiah 40, verse 31 gives us hope because, through it, God assures us that:

> *…they who wait for the Lord shall renew their strength. They shall mount up with wings like Eagles. They shall run, and not be weary. They shall walk and not faint.*

God always provides for what He asks us to do. That provision is rarely what we assume it will be; it rarely arrives ahead of time (or is that just me?). The problem usually begins as we lift onto our shoulders all those good things that need doing, which God never actually asked us to do.

'God is good, but not all that is good is of God.'

When we think about the Eagles, soaring high in the air, we know that the reason why they can travel such great distances is simply because they do virtually nothing in order to do so.

Eagles have fairly small muscles that they use to get into the air. But, once they're airborne, there is little for them to do once they find the thermals that they use to carry them high and far, other than to keep their wings locked in place and constantly check they're still riding a thermal of warmer air.

On one particularly super busy day – when I actually managed to follow my own advice for a change and ride those God given thermals – I didn't accomplish all that I had written down on my To Do list. I did, however, accomplish everything that God had wanted me to accomplish. The fruit from that day was my finishing it feeling refreshed for the next day, rather than frustrated and exhausted.

Sure, it took a little effort on my part, much like the eagle rising into the air to find a thermal. I had to spend some time working to focus on God, reading the Bible, spending some time in prayer with Him, and surrendering to God my own desires for all that I thought I should be doing. But, once I'd done that, I simply rode those thermals and accomplished more than I ever thought possible before I started.

Much like the majestic eagle, we shouldn't seek to work outside of those thermals, which I would describe as God's clear and comforting voice of peace.

If we walk in His strength; if we walk at His pace, and in His rhythm – and at His direction! – we "shall run, and not be weary. [We] shall walk and not faint."

Just a thought…

24. There's always something to be thankful for

Some days can be pretty interesting, can't they?! Today has been one of those days. I made my way through it the best I could, but I never felt especially brilliant, or even in control of what was going on around me. 'Interesting' was all I could come up with that evening when asked how my day had gone.

I had failed to get done what I truly thought I should have been easily able to get done. I had managed to press on through my day, nonetheless, despite the many obstacles that did their best to de-rail me and my day.

The next day was much better. As a family we managed to record another episode of one of our regular broadcasts – Endurance. The filming went really well, as did the rest of the day. Some new microphones arrived and were put straight to good use, which brightened my day because their higher quality was quickly obvious, and

I knew they'd save me loads of time when it came to editing later.

But that's life, isn't it? We all have good days and bad days. Although, and perhaps this is just me, some days feel like hybrid days – when the good and the bad days sneak up together and join forces against us, leaving us drained and confused.

The problem with letting our feelings guide us, or allowing our minds to wander too much, is that we can end up missing out on all those little wins that we each have every single day, like getting dressed in a groggy state, but still managing to come downstairs sporting a pair of matching socks; like brewing your first cup of tea without spilling too much of the gone off milk on your matching socks!

Like I said, little wins! But those seemingly insignificant, little victories can get lost in the sea of endless struggles and noises that always scream for our attention.

Yesterday wasn't a great day for me. It wasn't dreadful; it just wasn't good – I never got into the day, and it finished as frustrating as it had started. Swipe left just one day on your digital diary, and I was having a great day.

But what was on my mind? Not the good day! Oh no, just the less than stellar day I had endured yesterday.

It takes deliberate effort to focus on the good, because the bad is always more than willing to dramatically slap us across the face like a wet fish on a cold day.

So, if you're feeling overwhelmed today, take it to the Lord in prayer.

If you've forgotten to make your bed, which you stripped before leaving for work due to the coffee you dropped on it, didn't take any food out of the freezer and are forced to drink tap juice, because you didn't go to the shops to replace the gone off milk you dropped on your socks this morning, take it to the Lord in prayer. And maybe change your socks!

'Cos here's the thing:

You spotted that gone off milk and binned it – a win! You didn't end up with food poisoning – a bigger win (even if it did leave you without your morning hit of caffeine).

You wore socks that didn't match, but you had socks on – a win! Ok, they smelt, but at least you had socks on for that important meeting, albeit smelly ones, but nobody came close enough to notice – a bigger win!

You didn't react with hostility when the photocopier swallowed your tie as you lent over it to fix it – a bigger win!

You spilt coffee on your freshly laundered bedding – but you didn't scald yourself, and you saved your mattress from smelling of Brazil's finest blend of coffee beans for the next few months – a win!

Whatever your day looks like, take it the Lord in prayer. Look up, not down – you'll feel God's face shining on you!

The bad days always like to make you feel they're more important and the 'norm'. But they're just part of the rich tapestry, and there's always a flip side to everything that gets us down; there is always something to be thankful for, no matter what sort of day you're having.

Just a thought…

25. Don't Miss God!

I found myself reading a truly excellent Blog Post written by a good friend of mine. He was talking about how he had prayed for something, and how God had done something and then answered that prayer. He found himself thinking, 'Oh, wow, God actually answered my prayer.'

And it struck him that as often as he prays, it was far too easy to forget that God is actually the God of miracles, and that God really excels at doing amazing things! It's in His nature after all, because He made you, and He thinks you're amazing too!

While filming an Episode of Little Blessings Online, our online baby and toddler group, my wife – Jo - and I were thinking about Moses and the burning Bush. We went on to film a Story Time video too, with Dave the Dog – always good fun discovering Dave's unique perspective on things!

When we read the account of Moses hearing the voice from the burning bush, do we hear the bush speaking and think, 'Wow, isn't that an amazing bit of nature?' Or do we think of the voice of God, speaking in a miraculous way?

Often, in life, there's this 'stuff' that goes on, and we can miss who God really is. That's why it's always good to be thankful and to put ourselves right with God - so we don't get full of ourselves and end up pushing God out of our minds and hearts.

If we remember who God truly is and see a miracle unfold before us, we'll be able to say, 'Yes, this is of God; He's still good, and He still loves me!'

All of that got me thinking about Moses and that Bush, which tied in with my friend's Blog Post – about how we can pray for something, and yet still be totally surprised when God hears, and actually answers, our prayer. You know? Like we asked Him to do in the first place!

How often is that the case for you? How often do you pray, expect God to do something amazing, and then immediately forget you'd asked God to do the very thing He is literally just doing as a result of the prayer you literally just spoke? Tell me this isn't just an Andy B problem?

This week we've had some good days and some less good days. This week we've had some great filming days and some not-so-good filming days. But we've got upgraded microphones that work really well. And we've got mobile phones that are working really well as cameras for our filming.

And yet, throughout the week, I've been struggling with wondering whether or not we're wasting our time with our Online Ministry; I've been wondering about how I use my time and whether or not it is really being used well!

I'm still wondering whether He wants us doing the very thing He has just enabled us to do even better, again…I've missed the miracles of provision that we, as a family, have spoken to God that affirm just this.

Sometimes the solutions to the issues of life that we face may need a little effort on our part – God has designed us with amazing brains and intellect to deal with multi-faceted and complex issues.

But let's not miss the miracles carried out by the hand of God - especially when we've just prayed for something that is unfolding directly in front of us.

Let's not be so surprised when we pray to God, hoping He'll intervene, only to miss Him intervening because we're too busy wondering how that miracle happened...

Just a thought…

26. Plugged in and Not Switched On

I was working away on our laptop one day, busily beavering away - getting lots of stuff done.

Before starting, I set about plugging in the computer to the mains socket on the wall because, while our laptop has a pretty good battery life, it just makes good sense to plug it in when it is easy to do so. That way the next person who wants it has everything ready to go.

I plugged the mains cable into the back of the laptop and put the other end of the cable near the mains socket on the wall so I could plug it in.

And then, well, I got a bit distracted and, of course, didn't actually plug that mains cable into the mains socket on the wall before jumping onto the laptop to get some work done.

That got me thinking about our relationships with God, because God is always there, just like the mains power supply in my house – I'm very confident it is there and that it will always work as anticipated – power cuts are pretty rare where we live.

In the same way, I am even more certain and confident that God IS always there, with no lag or fluctuation to His provision of service!

God doesn't suffer from power cuts, broken transformers or being "Under Maintenance". He is always there and has an availability rate far exceeding just 24/7! His Customer Services are world beating.

And yet, if we pay the electricity bill and have a plug socket, or a mains socket, but only put the plug somewhere in the vicinity of that mains socket on the wall, it's simply not going to be the same as actually plugging it in! I know you can buy devices that use contactless recharging these days, but there is a limit even to that!

And this got me thinking about our Bible reading efforts; our prayer life – those times we set aside to deliberately spend with God.

Are we placing the 'mains cable' of our Spiritual walk simply near to the mains socket of God? Are we sitting there with our Bibles open, but not actually reading them - – perhaps just skimming them at best – while scrolling through Facebook for things we need to pray about (speaking for a friend……)?

Are we praying, but just going through the motions? Are we reading something from a book, or a journal, rather than actually fully engaging and actively praying both to

God and with God. And remember that good communication involves both speaking and listening!

Are we going to flick open our Bible and just see where the Holy Spirit leads us, or are we going to actually be strategic and purposeful, and have a proper reading or study plan, so that we can know what we're going to read and get on with it?

It's all too easy to have the mains charger of our Spiritual walk sitting right next to the unending power of God!

I had my laptop properly plugged in. I was merrily working away. It was only when an alarm on the laptop started beeping away at me that I realised there was something wrong, because I'd only plugged it in at one end. The battery was about to force the computer to switch itself off!

So, let's make sure that when we're spending time with God – whether that's reading the Bible, praying, or anything else – that we're not just putting ourselves somewhere near the endless power source of a relationship with Jesus. Let's ensure that we're actually fully plugging ourselves into that time.

The great news for us as Christians is that Jesus already paid ahead, and His credit is off-the-charts good! We won't have to risk losing access. All we ever have to do is simply turn up. Jesus takes contactless recharging to a whole other level, but we still need to turn up.

Just a thought…

27. Car Covers, Trees and Protection

We bought a cover for our car. While that may not sound like an especially exciting purchase to you, it was very exciting for us. I'd rather not have spent out on it, but it was still very much worth it!

I was thinking about our new car cover, because the car cover that we used before only just about covered the windscreen, but that was about all. But now, we are the proud owners of a full car cover.

So, what possessed us to make such an exciting purchase like this?

If you lived where we lived, and you had an enormous oak tree in your garden that hung over the entirety of the enormous drive – and your car – no matter what you did, you might have bought a full car cover too.

It's worth noting that this particular oak tree, aside from being, allegedly, a few hundred years old, is the perfect home to the UK's entire population of holidaying pigeons and their children. It also seemed to be rather popular as a bird maternity ward too! If that wasn't enough, oak trees – as we discovered – also produce an enormous amount of sticky sap, and I just didn't fancy cleaning the windows of the car every time Jo needed to leave for work anymore.

Once you factor in all of those elements, covering your car every day, all year round, makes a lot of sense. The little gifts those pigeons kept leaving on the car, no matter where we tried to park it, just couldn't be returned, and I had grown rather tired of their enthusiastic present-giving!

All of this got me thinking about our relationship with God, because, as we go through life, there are times when we want to be under God's protection.

There's even a lovely piece of Scripture which talks about exactly this which we can find in Psalm 17, verse 8:

> *"Protect me as the pupil of your eye. Hide me in the shadow of your wings."*

We all want to be under God's protection, don't we? Because it sounds like such a wonderfully good, comforting, and reassuring place to be.

This doesn't mean that once we get there all of our problems will suddenly disappear as we 'dwell in the shadow of the Most High'. Neither does it mean that we'll find ourselves protected from the same difficulties and persecutions that everybody faces every day – that is simply not the purpose and advantage of being under God's protection!

So, what's so good about living in the shadow of God?

Well, it's a place where we can find peace, in order to be who God is asking us to be for His kingdom. And that is what being under the shadow and shelter of the Most High God really means to me.

And that peace is always worth striving for and protecting! It's like a warm blanket on a cold morning – it just makes us feel better!

So, where in your life are you wanting to be in God's protection, but you know you're not? Where is it you know you're simply not surrendering those difficulties – which you know you can't handle yourself – to God?

If we truly desire to "dwell in the shadow of the Most High," then we simply need to give to God all of those things that we don't want; that we know we can't face on our own; that are burdens weighing us down to the ground.

God is more than big enough to shelter us from all of life's problems and worries. He doesn't shelter us from them so we never have to face them, although that will happen sometimes. He shelters us so we can know that the God behind us and over us is bigger than anything we will ever have to face with Him. And, to borrow a phrase from Master Samwise Gamgee, "that's worth fighting for."

Just a thought…

28. Calendars, Organisation And Peace

I was thinking quite a bit about diaries and calendars and organisation. You know – those things we easily forget to fill in and update; those things we forget to check or look at to remind ourselves where we were supposed to be an hour ago…gotta go…………..

While watching a video by Lauren Daigle singing one of her own songs, "You Say", I noticed that there was a girl in the video doing sign language.

It was a really beautiful thing to see. I cried!

She had clearly taken the time to be properly prepared, learn the song and the accompanying sign language – it flowed together seamlessly.

Her actions and her effort inspired me to think about how we can help others and what we can offer to others. This led me to thinking about how we have been trying to fit various things into our regular weeks as a family. It had gotten to the stage where we were simply left wondering how on earth we were supposed to fit everything in.

After much head-scratching, we returned to an older and much tried and tested system which we've used before.

To help us with having something of a fresh start I even bought a brand new, magnetic white board.

We then split it into 8 equally sized boxes using a permanent marker – one for each day of the week, plus a spare box for the overly used eraser!

We started by adding in which days Jo was going to be at work. We then started adding in all the other things we needed to be getting done. It all fitted together, and we found spare time to allocate for other things.

All of this organisation (which you may observe I rather enjoy) got me thinking about where it might be that God wants us to get more organised so we can have more time to give to Him.

Being organised would help eradicate all those wasted hours scrolling through Instagram reels.

I don't know about you, but I often look at my schedule and feel like it's just not gonna happen! However, we're never going to be busier than God wants us to be, unless we choose to.

God doesn't want us to be too busy, because that would be contrary to how He desires for us to live. He may have been busy handmaking the world over those first 6 days, but He also took time out every evening and on that 7th day.

When we get busier than God wants, we lose our peace; we get stressed; we get anxious.

When we factor in our working week; our time at school or college; our time at home – whatever your role might be – we can easily have too many things to try and fit in to the time we see before us.

So, how do we fit everything in?

On my busiest days, before I attack the day, I [try to] take time and write down everything I think is critical, and then I pray about that list.

Before long I'm usually crossing a number of those things out because, when placed under God's scrutiny, they suddenly lose their urgency as I allow God to help me rewrite my To Do list. And all of a sudden, my day seems quite possible.

What I've discovered, through much painful self-examination – and plenty of failure – is that having approached the day via God, I'm less stressed; I'm less anxious; I'm less frustrated, because I know that everything is covered in prayer.

As I do that, I keep hold of my peace, rather than throwing it away to meet a deadline that God never asked me to worry about.

So, where is God asking you to address this same situation in your own life? Where do you need to allow God to take a greater role in planning out your day?

If He can create the entire universe and everything in it in just 6 days, He can certainly help you – whatever your day may look like!

Just a thought…

29. Colanders, Saucepans and Strainers

We have a colander (or is it a strainer?). It's the thing you pour your vegetables into from a saucepan to drain AWAY the water.

I was thinking about how we strain things out of our life, because this particular colander is not my favourite! It's pretty good at many 'straining-type situations', but when we drain rice through it, we end up losing a bit of rice through the holes because they're a little too large!

If you're patient and strain your rice a little slower, you lose far less rice down the plug hole at the bottom of your sink. Conversely, if you're in a rush and get a little too enthusiastic, you lose loads of rice down your sink and have to pull it out of the drain by hand. So much time lost, all because you went a little too quickly!

I also have a saucepan and matching lid – a simpler, more basic way of straining. But, if you get the lid ever so slightly off when straining, you lose even more of your dinner into the sink.

Don't worry, this isn't turning into Ready, Steady, Burn!

In our lives there are many things we need to sift or strain. These may be things that we should be doing, or those things that we shouldn't be doing. But, either way, the best way of straining them is always going to be with the Bible. Obviously, I don't recommend using the actual pages as a filter!! But it is the standard by which we can measure anything. Or, carrying on my colander metaphor, it is the best tool for straining out those things we should be doing and those things we should not.

I measure all new colanders against the colander we no longer have – my favourite one, with perfectly sized little holes and a comfy handle. It even had straight sides, so you didn't end up with boiling water jumping out the other side!

My old colander is my standard for what I see as a good colander. But my Bible is the ultimate standard for everything else!

If we're thinking about how to strain things out of our lives that we know shouldn't be there – those character traits and natural tendencies that are simply not God's best for us, even if they're things that we think are good – the Bible is the very tool we need to work out how to separate those things from us.

The Bible is really the filter for every decision you will ever have to make in your life.

It never clogs or breaks or falls apart or runs out of the ability to function! The Bible is perfect every single time.

The Gideon bible is a great example of this, because it listed a whole selection of Scriptures for many of life's common struggles and situations, from worry to fear to mourning to love.

So, what is God asking you to strain out of your life? If you don't know where to start, or how to do that, you're in good company! But do ask the Comforter – the Holy Spirit – to help you. Invite Him to help you, open up the Bible, and see how God wants to remove from your life those burdens you don't need to be mixed up with anymore.

Just a thought…

30. Software, Updates and Change

Software and Change – those two words, especially when they're used next to each other, can instil a deep-seated panic and fear into even the most competent technology fans. Those two words can quickly magnify in our minds to become the reason why we fear we're going to lose everything that we hold precious on our computer, tablet, or phone.

It probably doesn't help that many updates have a warning added, suggesting that you back up, or save, all your information, just in case it gets lost! One way or another, we all use software, even if we're not consciously doing so, whether we're using a petrol station pump, emailing a friend, or even just making a phone call. Software is very much an integrated and essential part of our modern lives!

We do a lot of filming for the BerryBunch Ministry, and that inevitably leads to quite a bit of editing. Due to some changes with the audio editing software which we had been using, I was forced to seek out an alternative piece of software. I found one, and then I downloaded and installed it, and, actually, it turned out to be far superior to the software we had been using before!

I moved from a state of worrying about having to learn something new, to a state of being very glad about being made to change to the new software This is because it allowed me to automate many of the processes I had previously been doing manually!

Perhaps you've lost a job. You were going along through life in one direction, and you've suddenly had the rug pulled out from under your feet, and you've been forced to look for a totally new, unwanted direction.

We've had unemployment foisted upon us by some really unpleasant people, completely unnecessarily – they just wanted to be cruel to us and hurt my family. So, what do you do at that point? What is the correct response in that situation?

When we lost our jobs, we were badly hurt by that situation. However, we didn't ultimately crumble, because we had a Giant on our side; God sent us all sorts of people to help us through that time. Life got *really* tough for a while, but it didn't end us.

John 3 v 16 tells us that if we want to go to heaven, Jesus is the only way there. Without an ongoing relationship with Jesus Christ – as our Lord and Saviour – there is no way of getting to heaven. He truly is "the [only] Way, the [only] Truth and the [only] Life." Unless we allow Jesus Christ to operate in our lives and hearts, we will find ourselves frequently floundering in this life.

Life changes around us, and we all need regular downloads and updates – for the software of our minds – to help us navigate the ever-changing world around us.

If you let God update your mind and heart, you can be assured that you'll never have to fear losing any of the data that makes you who you are because of a corrupted update patch or dodgy connection.

Some things will look different, but always for our good! And if something does need deleting, it's always to make room for something much better.

I remember having to do a computer course on how to use a mouse. It was a brand new 'thing', and I thought it was dumb. Why use that funny looking thing when you can use a computer by just typing?

And then I started using one. It was such a game changer. Today it would seem odd not having that familiar little friend under our hand when navigating around a computer.

When I switched to a trackball mouse a few years ago, it was another game changer that felt odd at first. And yet, now, I couldn't simply go back to a regular mouse.

We can fight change, or we can embrace it – it's gonna happen whether we want it to or not!

Change can be scary, but it can also be oh so very good too! And changing to become more like Jesus is the sort of thing that always works out better for us. There simply is no downside. It's always a win-win for us and the people we love.

Are you willing to let God renew your mind and update the software that helps you decide how to live in this world?

Just a thought…

31. Keepin' on, Keepin' On

Have you ever heard the phrase "keeping on keeping on"?

Sometimes, it can be really hard to keep going through the busyness of life. Putting one foot in front of the other can seem to be a herculean task, and the idea of "keepin' on keepin' on" can seem too much to bear!

My wife, Jo, and I have frequently worked a 6-day week. It feels quite normal to us. From running our own business and working in full-time ministry, a 6-day week has been the 'norm' for large parts of our working life.

Jo had been working a 5-day week – Tuesday through Saturday – every week. And, while we've happily had Mondays as a family day off for a good number of years, working a 5-day week from Tuesday to Saturday never felt quite normal. It never felt quite right.

It always ends up super confusing when we finally reach Friday evening – the usual end of a working week – and realise we still have one more day before Jo, and the rest of us, can put our feet up.

By Wednesday we realise we're still not yet halfway through our working week, and it leaves us feeling rather perplexed, and somewhat out of sorts. And that's what led me to recall the phrase "Keepin' On Keepin' On".

All too often in life, there are things that try and prevent us from moving forwards – for bad or for good.

Some of those good things that can suddenly arrest our movement come in the form of seatbelts in a car! We'd have no complaints about them doing their job properly!

Some of those bad things might be not drinking enough and then wondering why we can no longer concentrate, think straight, or stand up. It's just our body reminding us to drink a glass of water. It's a really good thing, but we are rarely quite so grateful that our bodies have seemingly let us down!

The good news for us is that we can never be busier than we can handle when we keep on following God's gentle voice and clear leading. He'll simply never give us more than we can handle – with Him, because He will always equip us for the things that He wants us to do. His tactic is never to trick us into doing things. That is simply not in His nature.

The issue, of course, always comes when we mistake what He is asking us to do for what we think He is asking us to do.

As a society, we tend to associate Sunday as a rest day each week. Opening up Sundays as a normal shopping day in the UK was a dark day for everybody, as it removed an established day, and pattern, of weekly resting.

I love how The Entertainer (a high street toy shop in the UK) closes every Sunday to give all the staff a day off. It is no surprise to learn that the man at the top is a Christian. And God has blessed the decision to stay closed on Sundays! No surprises there though; 'God's plans are to prosper us,' and they are always for our best.

God took the 7th day off as a rest day. That 24-hour period of time was more than enough for Him to rest, having created an entire universe in the preceding 6 24-hour days.

So, our one day a week off should be more than ample as we don't have to balance the solar system or keep an eye on the hydrological cycle.

It's also worth reminding all of us to remember those folks who are employed to work in our churches on a Sunday.

It doesn't matter whether their function is that of a vicar, children's minister, worship leader, or any other role, their weekly day off is super precious to them too, just like yours is to you. So, make sure your respect their downtime.

Walking at God's pace often means letting go of some of those things that we tend to see as important, in order to give God the opportunity to show us what He sees as important. Otherwise, we just end up filling our days with things that might make us feel good but are of no benefit to us. 'God's plans are to proser us.' But if we want to see that prospering, we need to make sure we're following His design and plan for our lives.

Just a thought…

32. Never Give Up. Never Surrender!

I was recalling a number of conversations with a good friend of mine from Nigeria. Sometimes, we simply do not know if the things that we do have had an impact on somebody else. It can be hard to know if something we have done has encouraged or helped anybody else.

My friend made my world! When I was feeling a bit low, he told me that he had been watching one of my Andy B 2 Minute Videos, which had been inspired by the story of David and Goliath. My friend explained how much he had learned and how it had helped him in his own life.

When I create my Andy B 2 Minute Videos, they only ever happen when I've had an inspiration. I never force them to come to life. I don't craft or sharpen them. I simply record the original thought I had, so they remain as close to the original inspiration as possible.

I put all I am into them, but I frequently wonder if there is much point in making them.

Having put so much of myself into every video we produce, it's so very encouraging when I get some feedback from somebody saying "thanks". It is always certain to bring a smile to my face! So, if you're ever reading or watching something online, no matter who made it, hit that like button, or subscribe to their page – it means the world and helps us creative types!

The phrase "Never Give Up, Never Surrender" can mean all sorts of different things to you, depending on who you are.

If you're in my household, it can easily mean you're listening to a Christian rock band called Skillet again, in particular their track "Never Surrender". We love the band, and that song has a special place in our hearts; it is frequently being played somewhere in the house!

The other thing that the phrase "Never Give Up, Never Surrender" can conjure up is to do with a film called Galaxy Quest, starring Tim Allen and the late Alan Rickman, where this same phrase is also used.

But, if God has given you a vision, then go after it knowing that God will give you all that you need, because God always provides for whatever He is asking us to do for Him.

Keep telling yourself to "Never Give Up, Never Surrender" as obstacles, doubts, and plan-stopping pits pop up in front of you.

But don't ever expect God's provision to appear when you think it should. He always provides for us to accomplish the goals He has for us. But His timing is not our timing, so 'just in time' frequently looks different to what we hope it will.

If God is calling you to do something, do it with all your heart, but don't do it for others. Don't do it for more likes, or downloads, or comments, or whatever. Don't do it to complete the goal. Do it because God has called you to; do it because you love God; do it to build your relationship with God.

And remember: "Never Give Up. Never Surrender!"

Just a thought…

33. Whiteboards, Erasers and Faith

To try and make sense of everything we're each involved in, and to ensure that dinner is actually cooked at all – for the correct number of people at the right time – we use a whiteboard. You've surely heard the phrase "one whiteboard to rule them all." No? Well, we have that very whiteboard, and it hangs on a wall in our home.

If you want more of the exciting BerryBunch rock and roll, Middle Earth whiteboard lifestyle, you can flick back to Calendars, Organisation and Peace in chapter 28.

We use permanent pens to mark out all the things that are permanent, like the days of the week and the grid of 8 rectangles, so that we don't have to keep adding them when we rub out the previous week.

We also use magnetic paper, onto which we've printed commonly recurring activities, so that we can just move them about as needed. Non-permanent pens complete the proper organisational satisfaction of our whiteboard.

All of this stuff about our whiteboard got me thinking about how sometimes, when we're praying and walking with Jesus, we like to use a non-permanent pen.

When we're praying out loud to God, are we praying in a non-permanent pen, or a permanent pen?

Are we praying with the kind of passionate, unwavering belief that we can read about in James 1 – where we're encouraged not to be double-minded and tossed about like a wave of the sea? Are we praying in faith – with a permanent pen? Are we praying in a way that commits us to something?

Or are we very carefully praying in non-permanent ink?

Are we praying tentatively, perhaps even suggestively, to God about whatever need we may wish to bring to Him? It can almost be as though we expect our loving Heavenly Father to be uninterested in our needs, because they're not holy enough or something similar. So, we try and save face by praying in such a way that prevents us from sounding foolish; in a way that can be undone if needed. In a way that is like writing with a non-permanent pen, which can be quickly and easily erased from our memory.

When we pray, let's use a permanent pen. Let's ditch those tentative prayers, throw away those prayer-erasers, and say what we mean with passion and belief that we're speaking to a Father who cares about every single word we need to say to Him.

God is always willing to hear our prayer. But how willing are we to be inconvenienced in order to speak to Him?

In his book, The Cross and the Switchblade, David Wilkinson often talked about the importance of saying things out loud, because then you can be held to account. When we pray out loud, it's the same as writing with a permanent pen. If we pray silently, it's like writing with a non-permanent ink…just in case we need to rub it out later.

Let's invest in some permanent-pen-praying and pray out loud, believing God will do the amazing things that only He can arrange both in and through our lives – and the lives of others too.

It's great to have a non-permanent pen when writing in possible future plans. They will change, regardless of our effort or input. But let's use permanent pens when praying to God, and let's take ownership of the words we speak to God.

If we don't want them to be heard by other people, then perhaps we don't really want them enough to be heard by God either?

Say what you mean and mean what you say. Say it loudly and boldly with a hearty Amen! Who knows who might need to hear you speaking to a Father Who loves both you and them?

Just a thought…

34. Reading, Trembling and God

While having something of a chat with God over a weekend, I was led to read Isaiah 66, in the Old Testament of the Bible. Isaiah 66, verse 2 says this:

> *"All these things my hand has made, and so all these things came to be, declares the Lord. But this is the one to whom I will look – He who is humble and contrite in spirit, and trembles at my word."*

The general context for this particular piece of Scripture is that of God speaking of all the things He has been doing.

Isaiah 66, verse 1 is talking about the same thing we can also read of in Genesis chapters 1 and 2 – it's kind of like God saying, "Look here at everything I've already done." But, against the backdrop of God making the heavens and the earth and everything in them is His most treasured creation – human beings!

And of all the peoples on earth, who is God looking for the most? He is seeking those who are "humble and contrite in spirit."

If I'm honest I wasn't actually sure what contrite meant and had to turn to a dictionary to find out. I discovered that contrite means your heart is remorseful for the things you have done wrong.

But the thing is, we can't truly 'come to God' unless we are contrite and humble in spirit.

It's worth reminding us that God is not our mate, pal, or chum either. As Mr. Tumnus so wonderfully puts it in the Chronicles of Narnia, "He [Aslan] isn't a tame lion!" He is still God, and trembling at His word is not remotely suggestive of being afraid of who He is – it is about having reverence for who God is, as Lord of Lords and King of Kings.

In the first two chapters of the book of Genesis we have, in written form, God's own account of how He made the world and everything in it.

As you look through the rest of the Bible, you'll find a book for people who are married, or getting married, in the Song of Songs. You'll find the book of Psalms and its wondrous ability to turn your mood back to front, and turn that frown upside down.

Move on to the New Testament, and you can read about the life of Jesus Christ as He walked on the earth – from His birth to His death to His coming back to life and going up to heaven.

The Bible is 66 books of eternally useful teaching, and it's applicable for every single one of us – every single word of it!

God made some amazing animals. He set in motion the 4 Seasons. He designed mountains, animals, birds, fish, beaches, rainbows and even wasps – one part of His creation that I'd sure like to know a little more about!

And, far more important than anything else that God created is us – people, who He hand crafted in His own image. He speaks the world into being, but He makes us by hand. That shows us how much more important people are to God than animals, the environment, or anything else in the Solar System. He simply put too much attention and detail into us for us to be either equal or of lesser value to anything else.

People are who God values the most, and of all the people on the earth, God is looking for people who are trembling at His Word – people who are aware of their own failings; people who have already said sorry to Him for those things they get wrong before they come towards Him.

God loves you! He cares about you, and He cares for you.

So, tremble at His voice, but don't be afraid of Him – He made you in His own image with both purpose and intention.

Just a thought…

35. Planning, Preparation and Puzzles

We all think about the future in one way or another, whether we are thinking about what to eat for dinner, considering where we might hope to be on New Year's Eve, or even planning for our next holiday.

As a family, we have diaries. We have a mix of paper and digital ones, plus a whiteboard. They all help remind us of where we are supposed to be and what important things we need to be reminded of, like who is cooking dinner, and which day is pay day.

I don't know about you, but, quite often, life can feel like something of a puzzle. How do we get from A to B? How do we fit all of that in to such a short week? How are we going to accomplish everything we need to get done? And, sometimes, our days can become so busy that God simply gets squeezed out.

Filling in that whiteboard is always easiest when we start with the most obvious, unmoveable things, like those times when Jo needs to be at work. We move on to the side pieces – various activities that must be done before the weekend – and move on from there.

In life there are a lot of things for which we need to plan ahead. For example, if you drive a car in the UK, you have to arrange car insurance and an MOT (an annual check for vehicle mechanical soundness and roadworthiness). This means you need to book a garage in good time – ahead of that all-important date one year on from last year's form – so that the garage can fit you into their own diary and workload.

We were once reminded, by post, that the vehicle breakdown cover we pay for every year was about to expire. This is something else that needs dealing with ahead of time, so we don't risk Jo being stranded somewhere on her way home from work, at night, in the rain, with a car that doesn't work, and no breakdown recovery service standing by with mechanics ready to come to her rescue, something akin to the Thunderbirds!

Do we let ourselves have that same mentality about praying or spending time reading the Bible? Do we put as much effort and emphasis into being aware of things coming up and ensuring that what matters most – our daily time with God – is not squeezed out?

This is why I tend to think of organising the life of my own family as something akin to a jigsaw puzzle; we start by seeking out the corner pieces, before moving to the edges, so that we have a nice, clearly defined, firm boundary to work with and against. Everything then falls far more easily into place as a result.

Do you put as much effort into protecting your times of prayer and Bible reading as you do into ensuring your car is safe and legal to drive for another year? Do you treat those 'known factors' as the corner pieces that make up the rest of the jigsaw of life? Or do you end up throwing all of the pieces in the air, simply hoping they'll somehow simply fall in just the right place?

It takes effort to seek out those corner and edge pieces. But, when we put them in first, it helps everything else fit far more simply.

And it is the same with our prayer and Bible reading! When we put those most important elements in first, everything else always flows far more easily – and with far less stress or head-scratching!

Make sure you don't let God get squeezed out of your everyday life, because you forgot to see Him as the corners of the jigsaw puzzle that make up the days of your life.

Just a thought…

36. Habits, Peace and Feelings

In a conversation with one of my sons, I mentioned a man, Dr. Neil T. Anderson, who started an amazing ministry called Freedom in Christ Ministries. Neil had shared about why he had been led to create this particular ministry, as he'd seen such a great need to help people break free from habits that they just seemed unable to break free from, no matter how hard they tried or how much they wanted to be set free.

One of the things he regularly points out is how very easy it is to form a habit. You just need to do the same thing 6 times, and a habit can be formed. But, as he further explains, it can take 6 weeks of not doing that same thing in order to break that habit.

Making a habit is so much easier than breaking one!

I've also been reminded how incredibly fickle our emotions can be, changing over time so suddenly as they do. We might wake up in the morning feeling great about the day ahead, but that can change so quickly when a tyre on our car is flat, and we're already late for work. Those 'good' feelings disappear faster than the air from that tyre!

Just as our emotions constantly change, so too do our mood and our countenance. It's all too easy to be feeling flatter than a flat tyre in no time at all!

Our emotions change a lot, which is why we should never trust them to steer us in any of our decision making. They are a great temperature gauge for us to check out how we are doing, but they only give us one small glimpse of the whole picture. Our emotions are also very subjective – how we feel doesn't necessarily have anything to do with reality.

For example, when we go through puberty, the hormone levels in our body can change dramatically, whether we're male or female. The physical changes can be more obvious to recognise, but it changes us from children to adults. And, while puberty doesn't last very long, those feelings can be very strong.

I truly believe puberty is a wonderful gift from God, which He gives us to help us prepare for the rest of our lives – whether we're called to be single or married.

Puberty can be embraced as a great opportunity – when we tend to have no real responsibilities as yet – to learn how to recognise that our emotions can help us, but they can change too, and so they need to be treated with both respect and godly wisdom.

Jesus went through puberty too, which I find really encouraging. And He had emotions, including extreme emotions that most of us will never have to face.

But what has all of this about puberty and emotions got to do with peace? Well, if you're trying to find peace in who you are, in yourself, or in your situation, you need to know who you are in Jesus Christ - in order to find that sort of level and sustainable peace.

We can see ever increasing numbers of people drinking, taking drugs, and looking for anything that might enable them to find greater value and meaning in themselves, so that they can find and experience peace.

As a Christian I can state, with absolute certainty, that if you know Jesus Christ; if you follow Him; if you put yourself right with Him; if you make your heart reconciled to Jesus Christ, then you will find peace! In fact, the more we become more like Jesus, the more confident we will become of that peace, which is beyond understanding.

Emotions are important, and God made you with emotions for a reason – how we are feeling matters to God!

But don't let your emotions direct you to change who you are. While they're a great thermometer, they also change and we can mis-read our emotions, especially when hormones become more extreme such as during puberty or pregnancy.

If you want a peace that is sustainable and tangible, you need an ongoing relationship with God.

Give your feelings – and your future – to God, and He will guide you safely along the path ahead of you.

Just a thought…

37. God, You and Me!

I have a friend who lives in Scotland, in the UK. He writes amazing posts on his blog, which I find incredibly refreshing and challenging. And I have another friend who lives in the southeast of the UK. He's another blogger whose material I thoroughly enjoy reading.

And yet, on one particular day, these two writers published posts that were wonderfully connected to each other and my own journey of walking with Jesus.

Between them, even though they had had no contact about their posts on that one day, they were used by God to speak directly into my life about something I had been struggling with.

I love it when God does this – when He uses unconnected writings to connect to something in our heart, to help us become more like Jesus Christ.

This sort of encouragement is exactly as it should be. As Christians, we should be encouraging each other; we should be edifying one another – literally building each other up. While we're encouraging them, they are also encouraging us at the same time.

Between these two posts it was reassuringly clear that I was being asked to consider how I assess my efforts and progress. God was asking me to consider who I was writing our BerryBunch material for. Was it for people who I wanted to impress with my writing ability? Was it to get more likes and followers? Was it to make us look better than other online ministries? Or was it to make God smile at our efforts, as a family, to simply show others more of who He is?

In modern Christianity, we have been increasingly taught to see God as our best mate; our chum; our pal. And yet, sadly, this skewed understanding can then confuse how we see who and what the devil is, because it suggests that we have power over the enemy of our soul, which, of course, we don't have as people! In fact, as Christians, we need to acknowledge that it is only Christ in us who has power over the devil, not us.

We need to retain a healthy sense of reverence for who, and what, God is, because God is most definitely someone we should see as a friend we can approach, no matter what is going on in our lives, and no matter how well or how badly it is all going.

And yet, God is so much more than just a friend, because He is also our Heavenly Father. He is the Lord of Lords and King of Kings. He is Jehovah Jireh. He is also so much more than just those few titles.

God is not just the best of something. He is so completely set apart from comparison to all the good things that we could measure Him up against, because He is God; He is so much more than just 'good'. He's totally accessible and approachable too – something that larger church pastors and travelling preachers would do well to remember.

So, as you go through the coming days and weeks ahead, remember that God is God, and you need to approach Him with reverence – like the Heavenly Father and Creator that He is.

We should always want to come to God, our Father, and talk to Him. But we need to do so with a healthy dose of reverence for who God is, and an ease of coming to Him – no matter how we feel, or what is going on in our lives.

Just a thought…

38. Prayer, Reverence and Confidence

In the previous chapter I was talking about how modern Christianity has skewed how we see who God is and how we approach Him. I spoke of how this has also skewed our relationship with Jesus Christ and how we approach approaching God.

In a comedy video a friend shared with me, titled simply "How Nigerians pray", the video takes a humorous look at how Africans and Nigerians pray, especially when compared with how the rest of the world prays.

While it was sometimes a little awkward to watch, it was also very funny, because, as a Christian for more than 3 decades, I recognised too many of the ways they highlighted, like when one of the actors is shouting at God.

As human beings, we're often not all that interested in approaching God with a humble heart and seeking His will for our lives. We aren't always all that likely to ask God to show us where He wants us to be more like Him, because this approach usually ends up with us having to admit to pride and error in our lives, and none of us want those on display!

But God sees it anyway, which makes our trying to hide it even more of an interesting approach to our relationship with God. Why hide something from someone who, by their very nature, sees all, knows all, and is everywhere?!?

If we're honest, we're more likely to come 'at' God, while shouting 'at' Him for where He's failing to get things sorted the way we think they should be sorted in our lives.

What did Bruce Almighty do (in the film of the same name) as soon as he was giving God's powers? Yep – he went about sorting and improving his own life out first, and he didn't help a single person out despite having just accused God of doing the exact same thing.

When we're really honest, we're far more likely to make every effort to explain to God why He needs to take our advice, consider our position and situation in life, and do things more like we would. We all too easily just expect Him to be a god at our beck and call, rather than the Majestic and Sovereign God He truly is. Yes, Jesus came and lived, serving all of humanity. But we still serve God – He does not serve us!

The question we should be asking when we pray, however, is how God wants us to become more like Him, rather than when He is going to respond in the way we deem most appropriate.

Ever been praying and found yourself stifling the urge to tell God to just let you take the lead and simply back you up? Maybe that's just one of my prayers…

I'm sure God laughs at us saying such things as much as we do at a video we find funny.

Come to God with a humble heart and ask Him what his desires are for your life. Let's take the effort to put down our own opinions and critiques of God's handling of the problems we've faced, and let's let Him lead us, rather than trying to lead Him instead.

Come with a blank piece of paper, rather than a wad of To Do items God still hasn't yet accomplished for you.

God really does have a better perspective on our life than we do – so trust His view. It's so much better than yours ever can be, and He can see everything ahead of you that you cannot yet see.

What we see as a blurred dot in the future, God sees in all its high-definition detail.

Just a thought…

39. Heat, Tiredness and Hydration

Right now, where I live is suffering from a heatwave. A friend in Nigeria says a cooler day over there averages around 35 degrees centigrade. Personally, I've usually already melted if we're pushing north of 25 degrees!

I was speaking to my wife, and I stated that I simply couldn't cope with the heat any longer.

As a family, we had been doing all we could to stay cool. We were drinking plenty of water, keeping the curtains and blinds closed on windows that were facing the sun, and conversely opening curtains and blinds where the sun was absent.

We had fans on as necessary, circulating some air around the house and enabling us to sweat a little more easily in order to cool ourselves down.

And yet, as I spoke to my wife about how I could not cope any longer, I saw the usual recognition in her eyes that I had said something stupid again. It's not quite as rare an occurrence as I'd like to remember it to be.

As I said those infamous words "I can't cope anymore," my wife simply stated that I could. She helped me recall that, years earlier, I had driven trucks with cranes mounted onto them and delivered building materials.

She reminded me that, in the hottest part of the hottest seasons of a British summer, I would peel myself from the driver's seat and out of the greenhouse (that some people foolishly called a cab), stand in the baking sun, with multiple layers on, wearing a plastic hat, on top of the lorry engine revving away beneath me, in order to operate the controls for the crane, which some person had decided were best located next to the hottest part of the entire vehicle.

I can't think of many hotter places to stand on a hot day, and I could be up there for an hour or more at a time. So, if you see somebody delivering a load of bricks from a lorry, have a thought for them, and maybe offer them a cold glass of water!

In effect, I operated in an ambient heat of at least 30 - 35 degrees, with a giant fan blasting even hotter air right at where I was standing, and yet I would just carry on working.

And isn't that so true of life? How easily we can quickly forget how good we can be at something when we're failing at something else; how quickly we can forget our own abilities when faced with a difficult situation we've overcome many times before.

I still wasn't coping well with the heat, but I used to be able to work in the baking sun – in far worse conditions –

and still get the job done safely and proficiently and not pass out from dehydration.

How do we overcome heat exhaustion? We try and stay in the shade when the sun is at its hottest. Some countries deal with the heat by having a siesta, or a nap, when the sun is highest.

While we don't have the heat levels some countries do, here in the UK, you simply have to make sure you drink a little more, wear a hat to protect your head, and apply suntan lotion.

And, in addition to this, you also climb down from the back of your lorry, climb back into the greenhouse where the steering wheel for the lorry is situated, and get on with the job.

I never complained about it. That was simply the job! And I loved the job, if I'm honest – except having to peel myself from the driver's seat…that never got any easier!

In life, and in our lives as Christians, we can so easily forget how we were praying really well with God just a few hours ago. And when life gets hard, we can suddenly get so very negative and down and forget what God literally just did for us.

Let's have some hope and some peace.

If it's hot outside, get an extra drink of water and put a hat on. And, as Christians, let's keep going for God and for His Kingdom and do all we can not to forget all that God has already done for us.

Just a thought…

40. Struggles, Strength and Striving

I was discussing with a friend making difficult decisions. We were talking about the struggle of making decisions when life gets difficult and working out whether the hardship you are facing is you walking in your own strength, or just a difficulty of life that needs navigating.

Having been in full-time ministry, I would say that, for us, if something we wished to do had been inspired and was fairly easy to facilitate, then that was probably a good indicator of something God may be wanting us to do.

But it's also important to note that having the necessary resources doesn't mean that God wants us to do something.

Resources being in place too far ahead of time would make me very suspicious anyway, as that wouldn't help us learn much about becoming more like Jesus, relying upon God and walking in His strength, or doing something for His glory.

It's easy to do something if you have the money for it, but money simply doesn't equal approval from God.

And so, there I was struggling to make a difficult decision. Even the very thought about making that decision felt heavy upon my shoulders, so I asked a trusted friend to pray for me and give me some wise counsel.

I could not work out whether the burden I was feeling was because it was just a heavy burden that God wanted to help me carry, or if it was a burden that God did not intend for me to carry.

I'm the sort of person who likes to speak the truth in any given situation, rather than deliver it in a nicely wrapped package. And, sometimes, this has got me in to a bit of bother. Usually, if I'm honest, it's most likely because there are people in the room who need to hear something, and I'm more than willing to state the obvious…

And so it was that I once found myself in a side meeting at a Christian conference, in the UK, when I heard these words from someone else in the group, which sent shivers down everyone's spine and made people look for the EXIT sign:

> *"I'm so exhausted when I lead worship, and nobody thanks me, and it's terrible, and it's exhausting, and it's a thankless task, and I've got no inspiration for it – it just drains me every time I do it'."*

Those [PG edited] words were directed right at me and were, sadly, shouted at me with no small amount of venom and anger!

I had just been sharing how God always equips me, and all of us, to accomplish what He asks us to do. No big deal, right?

I had further explained that, conversely, if you are feeling exhausted by what you are doing, it is probably a good sign that something is not right, and you should probably stop and seek help and counsel from your church leaders. So, you can appreciate why that exhausted soul wasn't best pleased by what I'd just shared. However, their outburst rather well summed up what I'd been sharing.

If you're facing some striving in your decision making, or difficulties in your life that are preventing you from moving forwards, don't therefore assume that you need to stop. And, conversely, if it is really easy and you have resources spilling out of your pockets, make every effort to check in with God – the devil will always be ready to help us do something that God doesn't want us to do, and that includes giving us resources in order to run away from God's desire for our lives.

We frequently and routinely should be stopping and pausing to allow God the opportunity to more easily speak to us in a way we can hear.

God will never ask us to do something that is contrary to Scripture, and He will never force us to do anything or trick us into doing anything. God always wants our minds fully switched on and for us to be committed to what we're doing. He is after our hearts, not our hands. Get your heart right with God, and your hands will naturally follow.

So, go to God frequently – once an hour would be a good starting point – and double check you're walking in His strength, not your own.

Just a thought…

41. Roundabouts, Judging and Waiting

Things don't always go the way you hoped. Or at least they don't always go the way I hoped!

On a slightly overcast day, I decided to go out for a cycle on my mountain bike and go explore the beautiful countryside surrounding our home.

It was a lovely cycle, being almost completely off main roads. But the first and last parts involved a road and a small roundabout.

This particular roundabout must have been imported from the Hobbits of the Shire, as it was nothing much more than a biggish blob of paint on the road.

Having enjoyed the cycle, I had just a few minutes left before I arrived home. One right hand turn, a short bit of road, and I would be at home!

As I approached the small roundabout, I signalled my intention to turn right, as I always did, and I pulled over to the righthand side of my lane (in the UK, we drive on the lefthand side of the road – otherwise known as the correct side).

Nearing said roundabout, from the road ahead and to my left, was a man on a motorbike, and some other traffic behind him.

With the road laws being what they are over here, I knew it was my right of way, so I carried on, especially when I saw the man on the motorbike slowing down to let me pass in front of him, having looked long and hard in my direction.

I entered the roundabout satisfied that the biker had seen me, and was behaving as he should. So, I was rather shocked when he started screaming at me as he came to a very sudden stop.

He pointed, screamed, gesticulated, swore, and became very hostile and angry, because I supposedly hadn't given him any notice of what I was doing.

However, I noticed that he was wearing an only partially open helmet, with the majority of the front visor obscuring his vision: this is illegal in the UK. He couldn't actually see that I was in front of him until I was literally just in front of him.

What really upset me was that his anger was due to his own actions, not mine. I'd clearly signalled what I was doing, but when you ride with your face covered by your visor, because you didn't pull it down properly, you're gonna end up looking stupid when you can't see what's in front of you and you potentially kill or injure someone!

As a biker (and cyclist) myself, and a as professionally trained driver of many years' experience of all things very big, long, and heavy, I had no sympathy for him after his ridiculous bout of anger and the embarrassment he then felt due to his own actions.

That situation got me thinking about how we judge situations. It got me thinking about how, sometimes, what we see is actually not necessarily what we see!

If that biker had been riding to any reasonable standard, he would have had his helmet on properly, and he would have been far more able to easily see everything around him. He wouldn't have made a fool of himself, and he wouldn't have nearly ridden over me and my bicycle!

On a motorbike, you're trained to ride confidently but defensively, protecting yourself at all times. This means you need to have a good field of vision and be aware of what is around you at all times. Everybody wins, because this protects others too.

Riding defensively means you don't go around hurting others, because you're aware of your presence and how that affects others. It helps you not to do anything dangerous or foolish, because you acknowledge that you can't see everything, and you ride accordingly.

I felt for that biker, because his actions brought shame upon him; his anger is something he would have had to deal with and will have to answer to God for one day.

That could all have been avoided if he'd simply been riding safely and properly.

Let's not go around with obscured vision, shouting at people for the mistakes they're making when, all the while, we're the ones actually causing issues for others.

Just a thought…

42. Habits, Trusting and Change

I found myself needing to carry out some maintenance to my mountain bike. I enjoy doing the work, but it is always exciting putting a brand-new, shiny part onto my bike. I do this very rarely, as I repair parts more often than I replace them.

One of those parts that I had to replace is called a derailleur. This is a super important part on a bike. It's often taken for granted, but without it you can't change gear. So, it does matter if it works well or not!

In the simplest of terms, the derailleur hangs down from one side of your wheel. It's made of two smaller cogs (jockey wheels) that your chain passes over, and they keep the chain in tension, so it works properly. When you want to change a gear on your bike, you simply move your gear selector and this, in turn, allows the cable attached to your derailleur to move – so it can move either closer or further from your rear wheel – thus changing the gear you are riding along in.

When set up correctly – and when it is working well – one small click with your thumb can make this engineering marvel move just the right amount to change just one gear at a time. Mine wasn't doing that, so I assumed it was broken.

I've had the same problem with it ever since I bought my second-hand mountain bike some 5 or 6 years ago. The bike felt great and really well balanced, needing a little work, which I was happy to undertake. It was also really light, as bikes go, and did not look pretty! This was great as it meant it was less likely to ever get stolen.

I had a cycle shop replace a few parts that I didn't fancy replacing myself, and the bike just kept getting better. And, yet, this problem of changing gear persisted, no matter what was replaced. When I tried to change gear there was usually a banging sensation and some unpleasant noise as I changed gear – from both the bike and from me!

Memory can be a difficult one though. Not because we forget, but because we can remember some things far too well. We can remember things that are not there anymore.

I knew that when I next went out for a cycle, even with a brand-new derailleur fitted to my bike – correctly – it would take some time before I became fully confident in my bike not having that same issue. I had to learn to un-learn what I knew, which was no more.

That memory retention is the same issue we have with breaking habits, because a habit can form in just 6 repeats of an activity. However, it can take up to 6 weeks of not doing that same thing in order to undo that same habit – in order to break that habit.

It's going to take me some time to undo that habit of nervously changing gear, and so it is with life too.

We get used to something the way it is, we start to trust it, and then something changes – for good or for bad – and we then have to trust that what once was is not an issue anymore!

It takes us time to readjust from what was to what is. And in our relationship with Jesus Christ, we sometimes have to let go of the past in order to move into the future.

As we grow closer to Jesus, we have to let go of who we were, in order to become more like Jesus Christ, and that change doesn't happen overnight.

If it can take 6 repeats to form a habit, and 6 weeks to undo that same habit, we shouldn't be surprised when we struggle to suddenly stop doing something we know is wrong but have done all of our lives.

The good news is that, in around 6 weeks, we can undo any of those habits we've formed over years or even decades.

Sometimes God will help us to stop doing something immediately. I've seen it, and I've experienced it personally. But, more often than not, we simply need to keep putting one foot in front of the other and learn to trust that what is behind us is truly behind us.

Just a thought…

43. Identical but Different

This is part of a miniseries on me maintaining my mountain bike. There is much I learned about our relationships with God through the repairs I have had to undertake, which I wanted to share.

In particular, one part I had to replace was my bike's derailleur. If you're not sure what that part is on a bike, have a glance over the previous chapter: "Habits, Trusting and Change."

Many years ago, when my youngest son was 5 years old, we'd been to church one Sunday morning, as a family. As we were driving home again afterwards, he started saying, as only a 5-year-old can, that there was something wrong with the sermon; that "it just wasn't right."

Peter had made the decision that he wanted to become a Christian some 18 months earlier, and he was absolutely right – there was indeed something quite wrong with what had been spoken in that sermon, and he had picked it up, and the Holy Spirit in him had alerted him to it.

Like he said, it just wasn't right!

I knew something was wrong with my bike because something was quite clearly wrong. I had had various parts replaced that could have been the issue, but I still hadn't known what was causing to my pedals to 'bang', as they randomly did.

I eventually called up a local bike shop for some advice and, to be honest, was quite ready to book it in and pay for them to find and fix the problem. I'd run out of ideas!

He asked me what was happening and how old the bike was. He then asked for the name of the model of derailleur – printed on the outside of the metal housing – and immediately stated that I had the wrong derailleur fitted to my bike.

It took all of, perhaps, three to four minutes from me picking up my phone to call the bike shop, to my being confidently told what the issue had been all along.

It transpired that my bike had 8 gears for the rear wheel, and yet the derailleur fitted was only suitable for a bike with 9 gears, hence my struggle.

As Christians, how do we know the truth? How can we know the source of truth?

With a bike part, we go to a bike shop. That's where an expert can be found. When I called in – that same day – they handed over the part I needed. I fitted it as soon as I got home, and the problem I'd had for so many years was gone.

When it comes to everything else, we have even easier access to the true source of all knowledge: the Bible.

It is God's Word; the Bible even tells us that every single piece of writing within it is valuable to us and useful for teaching us how to live.

As we move along through life, we will always have those moments when, just like my son, Peter, we'll find ourselves saying "that is just not right".

But how do we deal with that? Well, we simply go to the one true source of knowledge; the plumbline: the Bible.

If you're feeling like something isn't quite right, then check it against the Bible, just as a builder uses a plumbline to check if a wall is straight. The weight on the end of that string hangs perfectly vertically, so it is easy to check if a wall is straight or not.

It's often said that while it is usually fairly easy to see the difference between right and wrong, it can be really hard to spot the difference between the nearly right and the nearly wrong. I'd agree!

So, if you're finding yourself not sure whether something is right or wrong, or nearly right or nearly wrong, check it out with your Bible. And if you can't find the answer that you're after, go find someone who's been a Christian for a while, and ask them.

Just a thought...

44. Rejecting Acceptance

God taught me loads with a spate of bicycle maintenance, and there's so much good learning in there that I'll carry on sharing what I learned – sometimes painfully – so you don't have to!

The problem I had been experiencing on my mountain bike had been happening for more than 5 years, and it was due to my bike having the wrong derailleur. It was random and always caught me off guard. But it also hurt, and I stubbornly figured I'd eventually sort it, and all would be well.

However, I had also come to the point where I simply had to accept that I had a problem that needed sorting, and that I could not deal with it myself. I literally had to "Reject [my] Acceptance" of what was.

For a long time, I'd simply accepted what I shouldn't have accepted. I'd somehow concluded that, well, that was just the way it was; that as I'm cycling along and start to put more pressure on the pedals, like when I'm going up a hill, the chain is going to bang from one cog to another – always bouncing my feet off the pedals. I'd accepted that was just the way it was going to always be with my second-hand mountain bike.

But how often do we do this in life? How often do we accept all sorts of things that we simply should have rejected, not accepted?

There are things that are not good or healthy, which we simply allow to continue and accept just as they are. It doesn't have to make sense – we simply learn to accept what we should reject. We become, in effect, comfortable with the uncomfortable.

Sometimes, it's wise to accept that we can't change something, but I wonder how many situations could have gone differently if I'd simply not accepted what I first saw.

Rejecting Acceptance is a healthy approach to life. When we're stuck or struggling, we simply need go to God in prayer and ask Him where there are things in our life that we simply need to stop accepting – like being unable to ever stop smoking; like never being able to lose weight; like knowing we'll always be alone and isolated. Those are lies which are not true, but it's oh so easy to believe they are as they are and cannot be changed.

For me, I'd simply become accustomed to the issue with my mountain bike. It was all due to one small part that was easily replaced, and the whole situation was resolved with the outlay of a tiny amount of money and a few minutes of my time.

Once I had replaced that part, my problem was all gone!

The Bible tells us that we are supposed to renew our minds every day in order to grow closer to God. We're supposed to walk towards Him as we become more like Jesus and less like who we used to be. And that means rejecting things that we've accepted, which we know we shouldn't have done. It means letting go of what we know 'is' and learning to accept what 'can be' instead.

So, where are you accepting something that you should be rejecting? Where do you need to exercise some 'Rejecting of your Acceptance'?

Talk to God about it, and He'll show you what to do if you ask Him.

It might take a few minutes of your time for it to be gone forever. It might be a life-long struggle, but one that God uses to help others find peace in their own lives.

Just a thought…

45. Wisdom Trumps Experience

One of the great things about the Bible is that it gives us something that never changes. God is the same "yesterday, today, and forever." This means that the Bible is something we can definitely put our trust in to help us check whether or not what we're doing is good.

It is so very easy to skip over those passages of Scripture that we either just don't easily understand or simply find a little – or a lot – uncomfortable.

Sometimes, we just avoid those passages that we find boring and dry, or simply don't like.

And yet God tells us that all of Scripture is useful for us, so there are, therefore, no boring bits; no dry bits; no bad bits – it is all good, especially those parts we'd rather avoid!

The whole beauty of becoming more like Jesus is not to find a way of making the Bible mould around us, but for us to mould ourselves around the Bible – around Jesus.

In the simplest terms, it is us who need to do the changing. And yet, how often would we rather just take a pair of scissors to the Bible to make it easier to read. But, if we did that, we'd end up cutting away more than just the parts we don't like, and that's the reason why we need to take it just as it is – all of it!

Reading the Bible can give us some good knowledge. But gaining that knowledge pales into insignificance when we learn God's wisdom. It's even better when we apply it.

Ever wondered why we still have Leviticus or Numbers in the Bible? They are full of rich resources which shape everything we may like to read in the New Testament. Let's never forget that the writers of the New Testament didn't have the New Testament – they only had the Old Testament. So, if you'd rather prefer reading the New Testament only, just remember that those writings are inspired by the words from the front of the book!

I thought the defective part on my bike was supposed to be where it was. It was there when I bought that bike second-hand, and it didn't look defective. In fact, it wasn't defective – it was just the wrong part for my particular bike.

At some point, somebody probably thought it was the right part too. And it may well have worked for a while, but it was only ever going to get worse the more it was used.

"Factory Fresh" means you're using the right parts that would have been used in the factory where that 'something' was put together. We trust that, at some point earlier, designers and engineers chose the right parts to function together best, testing that they all worked together well and fluently.

I knew there was something wrong with my mountain bike. However, in the end – and after struggling for a long time with something that should have worked – I went to somebody who knew more than me, a bike mechanic.

He told me it was the wrong part, because, while his experience helped me work out what the problem could have been, it was his wisdom that told me what it was; it was his wisdom that was able to discern between the possible causes and the actual cause.

Wisdom trumps experience, every time. And while human wisdom can be great, godly wisdom is always so much better.

So, who can you share some wisdom with this week?

Just a thought…

46. Coiled Potential Can Hurt!

If this was a video, you'd be looking at a picture of my thumb, slightly swollen, with a big plaster on it. Because I discovered the wrong way that Coiled Potential Can Hurt! Like, an awful lot!

Over the years, I've seen plenty of examples of parents raising their children. And it's quite normal for them to restrict their children from various things – in order to protect them. As parents we did it too. We still do it; it is a very good thing to stop our children from unnecessarily hurting and injuring themselves. Whether because we're taller, or simply older and wiser, we can see dangers that those younger or shorter than us cannot so easily see.

On the surface of it, this sounds like the best practice for raising children, because preventing a child from touching a fire is clearly a good thing, as is preventing them from running around the house so they don't slip, bang their head on the door catch, and need taking to hospital to have the gash on their head glued back together by a doctor. Likewise for leaving their toys in the middle of the hall so other people fall over them and end up treading on an expensive mobile phone. And, yes, all those examples happened to the BerryBunch family at some point.

While that strategy can be great, especially with younger children, there is also a built-in flaw to this approach that grows the more we use it. The problem lies in the fact that the more you squash or suppress something or someone, the greater the likelihood that that same suppression is going to be dramatically released, just like the coiled-up spring on my derailleur. Somethings need to experience a little suppression. But it needs applying wisely and carefully.

I ended up hurting my thumb quite badly because of that coiled potential, which I actually generated myself as I squeezed the derailleur to make it fit where I wanted it to go.

I damaged my thumbnail really badly, and I had to live with a blood-filled glove and a shattered nail that took ages to heal and stop throbbing.

Puberty is designed by God for each one of us to move through, as we move from being a child to being an adult. Jesus would have worked through puberty just like the rest of us – and that is an encouraging thought!

Puberty can be a time of extreme emotions. The way we see ourselves changes, and it can be very confusing without mature guidance to help us learn how to keep trusting in Jesus.

Puberty is the perfect time to learn to depend more upon Jesus; to 'lean into Him' as we face things that can appear so very overwhelming.

Reckless actions, excessive drinking, drug taking, and sex outside of marriage are examples of that coiled potential being dramatically released. However, it doesn't need to be so.

Alcoholism can be overcome. Drug taking can be beaten. Reckless living can be channelled. Sex outside of marriage, while never God's best intention for anybody, can also lead to the creation of another person, and a baby should always be both protected and nurtured – abortion is never the solution for the creation of another life.

Be careful when you're squashing someone that you simply want to protect. It's a great short-term strategy, like grabbing a child by the arm when they've innocently wandered into a busy road. But teaching them why they need to be more careful is always better.

And, if you're changing a derailleur on your bike, make sure you have a tight grip before squeezing it, because those little springs are far more powerful than they look!

Just a thought…

47. Fit for Purpose

My experience of replacing a defective part on my mountain bike has certainly been an interesting little journey for me! It all took place because someone, at some point, replaced a part with one that was sort of the right type of part, but not exactly the right part.

Sometimes you can get away with that, but with a bicycle derailleur, it's got to be right! It's either fit for purpose, or it isn't.

To be fair, it was, sort of, the right part. It was made by the correct manufacturer, fitted where it needed to be just fine, and it mostly worked. But, however close it may have been to being 'right', it was not right, and it was never going work properly.

Suffice to say that a derailleur is a critical component on a bicycle with gears. Without it gear changing stops being an option. Or, as in my case, it becomes a wholly nerve-racking affair! Because my bike has 8 gears, and this derailleur was designed for a bike with 9 gears.

As Christians, we need to be fit for purpose for God! Thankfully, if we walk with God, that's actually a fairly straightforward process – we just read the Bible and follow the Maker's instructions.

It doesn't matter if we kind of look right, if we kind of go to church, and if we kind of read the Bible. We actually need to be fit for purpose!

You wouldn't turn up to your new job working in a factory –which has a mandatory policy on wearing hard hats and steel-capped boots – while wearing your summer flip-flops and a baseball cap.

Flip-flops may be argued by some to be footwear. A baseball cap may cover your head, but a hard hat offers protection that your baseball cap cannot. And steel toe cap boots really do keep your feet safe, as my toes can attest – multiple times.

In our working life we need to turn up, fit for purpose. And it is no different with living out our Christian faith.

But how do we do that when it comes to being disciples of Jesus Christ?

One thing we can easily do is renew our mind every day, as the Bible tells us to. We can spend time with other Christians, especially those who have been walking with Jesus – whatever their age. We can have a humble heart and be willing to receive advice and wisdom, and we can be willing to give out wisdom too.

As somebody who is very passionate about the importance of godly marriages, I have grown ever more passionate about supporting others into ever more godly marriages, because people simply do not pass on advice, guidance, and wisdom as they used to.

With the growth of the internet it has become all too easy to become overwhelmed by the vast swathes of conflicting advice, either from people who simply want to make money out of you or, at the other extreme, people who genuinely care.

This can result in inaction, or with us simply following the one who shouts the most, or seems the most popular.

We have become accustomed to soaring divorce statistics around the world, because younger couples are far less likely to seek out more mature couples to guide them through their marriages.

For example, very few people are aware that it is quite normal to contemplate divorce around the 12 to 24 months period of marriage, as the initial rush of hormones from the start of that sexual relationship wane. That can 'feel' like the end of the world, when it is simply the moment to find another gear that will keep you going 'unto death us do part'. It's part of growth for a marriage.

We live in a broken world, full of broken people who all need hope. As Christians, we have access to the one single source of hope: Jesus Christ.

We so need to be fit for purpose!

Take time to seek out advice from mature Christians. Get into reading the Bible every day. And, whatever you do, make sure you keep praying and listening to the Holy Spirit, who will help you – and every one of us – each and every day.

Just a thought…

Broken Dreams, and Hope!

Andy B gets raw, and real, in Broken Dreams, and Hope!

Through the many difficulties he has faced, and his many broken dreams, there is one thing that always keeps his head above the water - hope!

And it is a hope that can not be quenched, no matter what life throws at him, or anybody.

"It is a page-turner in that sense, with each chapter leaving you wanting to read just one more..."

Introduction to the book

Are you hurting inside?

Are you left wondering where hope will come from?

Do you feel different from everybody around you – like you've got struggles they wouldn't and couldn't understand?

We're all looking for something to help us feel peaceful, and we'll do it any which way we can.

But there is one certain place we can find hope. And that is in a relationship with Jesus Christ.

Andy B gets raw and real in Broken Dreams, and Hope! Through the many difficulties he has faced, and his many broken dreams, there is one thing that always keeps his head above the water - hope!

And it is a hope that can not be quenched, no matter what life throws at him, or anybody.

Andy B is a gifted children's worship leader, speaker, teacher and preacher who loves exciting people in their faith.

He and his wife - Jo - live, and love, to help Families Fire Up Their Faith! They've been married for 25 years and have three godly men they're privileged to call sons.

You can buy Broken Dreams, and Hope! in paperback, or digital eBook, format, from Amazon.com

The BerryBunch

The BerryBunch.family website is an Online Ministry that provides video Resources to any, and all, that need them. As a family we work together to bring you home grown resources,: Like it, Share it, Download it, Use it!

Fire up your faith, with the BerryBunch: for free, for all!

From Dave the Dog to Endurance; From Marriage Matters podcast to Family Prayer Time and SO much more, there are hundreds of videos, and many hundreds of posts, all designed to resource you, encourage you, uplift you and be used by you.

www.BerryBunch.family

Printed in Great Britain
by Amazon

10872441R00102